Workshop on Extracting and Using Constructions in Computational Linguistics 2010

Held at NAACL HLT 2010

Los Angeles, California, USA
6 June 2010

ISBN: 978-1-61738-677-0

Printed from e-media with permission by:

Curran Associates, Inc.
57 Morehouse Lane
Red Hook, NY 12571

Some format issues inherent in the e-media version may also appear in this print version.

Printed by Curran Associates, Inc. (2010)

For permission requests, please contact the Association for Computational Linguistics at the address below.

Association for Computational Linguistics
209 N. Eighth Street
Stroudsburg, Pennsylvania 18360

Phone: 1-570-476-8006
Fax: 1-570-476-0860

acl@aclweb.org

Additional copies of this publication are available from:

Curran Associates, Inc.
57 Morehouse Lane
Red Hook, NY 12571 USA
Phone: 845-758-0400
Fax: 845-758-2634
Email: curran@proceedings.com
Web: www.proceedings.com

Introduction

A construction can be defined as a form-meaning pairing in which the components cannot entirely explain the meaning of the whole. Constructional phenomena range from morphemes to argument structure, and include obvious examples like collocations ("hermetically sealed"), (idiomatic) expressions with fixed constituents ("kick the bucket"), expressions with (semi-)optional constituents ("hungry as a X"), and sequences of grammatical categories ([det][adj][noun]), as well as more complex constructions involving, e.g., the occurrence of sentence composition features (e.g. transitivity) or adverbial types (e.g. spatial adverbials). As these examples demonstrate, constructions are a diverse breed, and constructionist theories do not give a government to any specific level of language. On the contrary, all levels are viewed as equally important.

Constructions are currently enjoying considerable attention in linguistic research, and are now widely considered as being much more frequent and central to language than what has traditionally been acknowledged. Constructionist theories emphasize that the human mind seems to prefer to use prefabricated chunks of linguistic elements (i.e. constructions) when possible, instead of generating sentences from scratch as in the generative grammar approach. Constructions are also gaining a central place in different kinds of computational linguistics applications; examples include machine translation, information retrieval and extraction, tools for language learning, etc. Constructions are an interesting and important phenomenon because they constitute a middle way in the syntax-lexicon continuum, and because they show great potential in tackling infamously difficult computational linguistics tasks like sentiment analysis and language acquisition.

This workshop encouraged submissions in all aspects of constructions-based research, including:

- Theoretical discussions on the nature and place within (computational) linguistic theory of the concept of linguistic constructions.
- Methods and algorithms for identifying and extracting linguistic constructions (collocations, idioms, multi-word expressions, grammatical constructions, etc.).
- Uses and applications of linguistic constructions (machine translation, information access, sentiment analysis, tools for language learning etc.).

The program committee accepted 6 papers that cover topics such as resources for constructions-related research, machine learning techniques for identifying constructions, using constructions to improve natural language processing applications, as well as studies of more specific constructional phenomena (e.g. verb-argument constructions, and presentational relative clauses). Each submission was reviewed by two members of the program committee.

We would like to thank the members of the program committee for their efforts, and the authors and presenters of the accepted papers for their high-quality contributions.

Magnus Sahlgren and Ola Knutsson

Organizers:

Magnus Sahlgren, SICS
Ola Knutsson, KTH

Program Committee:

Benjamin Bergen, University of Hawaii, USA
James Curran, University of Sydney, Australia
Stefan Evert, University of Osnabrück, Germany
Charles Fillmore, University of Berkeley, USA
Jonathan Ginzburg, King's College, UK
Adele Goldberg, Princeton University, USA
Stefan Th. Gries, University of California, USA
Matthew Honnibal, University of Sydney, Australia
Jussi Karlgren, Swedish Institute of Computer Science, Sweden
Krista Lagus, Helsinki University of Technology, Finland
Olga Lyashevskaya, University of Tromsø, Norway
Laura Michaelis-Cummings, University of Colorado, USA
Anatol Stefanowitsch, University of Bremen, Germany
Suzanne Stevenson, University of Toronto, Canada
Peter Turney, National Research Council, Canada
Jan-Ola Östman, University of Helsinki, Finland

Table of Contents

Workshop Program

Sunday, June 6, 2010

08:45–09:00 **Introduction**

09:00–09:30 *Towards a Domain Independent Semantics: Enhancing Semantic Representation with Construction Grammar*
Jena D. Hwang, Rodney D. Nielsen and Martha Palmer

09:30–10:00 *Towards an Inventory of English Verb Argument Constructions*
Matthew O'Donnell and Nick Ellis

10:00–10:30 *Identifying Assertions in Text and Discourse: The Presentational Relative Clause Construction*
Cecily Jill Duffield, Jena D. Hwang and Laura A. Michaelis

10:30–11:00 **Break**

11:00–11:30 *StringNet as a Computational Resource for Discovering and Investigating Linguistic Constructions*
David Wible and Nai-Lung Tsao

11:30–12:00 *Syntactic Construct : An Aid for translating English Nominal Compound into Hindi*
Soma Paul, Prashant Mathur and Sushant Kishore

12:00–12:30 *Automatic Extraction of Constructional Schemas*
Gerhard van Huyssteen and Marelie Davel

Towards a Domain Independent Semantics: Enhancing Semantic Representation with Construction Grammar

Jena D. Hwang[1,2] **Rodney D. Nielsen**[1] **Martha Palmer**[1,2]

[1]Ctr. for Computational Language and Education Research
University of Colorado at Boulder
Boulder, CO 80302

[2]Department of Linguistics
University of Colorado at Boulder
Boulder, CO 80302

{hwangd,rodney.nielsen,martha.palmer}@colorado.edu

Abstract

In Construction Grammar, structurally patterned units called constructions are assigned meaning in the same way that words are – via convention rather than composition. That is, rather than piecing semantics together from individual lexical items, Construction Grammar proposes that semantics can be assigned at the construction level. In this paper, we investigate whether a classifier can be taught to identify these constructions and consider the hypothesis that identifying construction types can improve the semantic interpretation of previously unseen predicate uses. Our results show that not only can the constructions be automatically identified with high accuracy, but the classifier also performs just as well with out-of-vocabulary predicates.

1 Introduction

The root of many challenges in natural language processing applications is the fact that humans can convey a single piece of information in numerous and creative ways. Syntactic variations (e.g. *I gave him my book.* vs. *I gave my book to him.*), the use of synonyms (e.g. *She bought a used car.* vs. *She purchased a pre-owned automobile.*) and numerous other variations can complicate the semantic analysis and the automatic understanding of a text.

Consider the following sentence.

(1) They hissed him out of the university

While (1) is clearly understandable for humans, to automatically discern the meaning of *hissed* in this instance would take more than learning that the verb *hiss* is defined as "make a sharp hissing sound" (WordNet 3.0). Knowing that *hiss* can also mean "a show of contempt" is helpful. However, it would also require the understanding that the sentence describes a causative event if we are to interpret this sentence as meaning something like *"They caused him to leave the university by means of hissing or contempt"*.

The problem of novel words, expressions and usages are especially significant because discriminative learning methods used for automatic text classification do not perform as well when tested on text with a feature distribution that is different from what was seen in the training data. This is recognized to be a critical issue in domain adaptation (Ben-David et. al, 2006). Whether we seek to account for words or usages that are infrequent in the training data or to adapt a trained classifier to a new domain of text that includes new vocabulary or new forms of expressions, success in overcoming these challenges partly lies in the successful identification and the use of features that generalize over linguistic variation.

In this paper we borrow from the theories presented by Construction Grammar (CxG) to explore the development of general features that may help account for the linguistic variability and creativity we see in the data. Specifically, we investigate whether a classifier can be taught to identify constructions as described by CxG and gauge their value in interpreting novel words.

The development of approaches to effectively capture such novel semantics will enhance applications requiring richer representations of language understanding such as machine

Proceedings of the NAACL HLT Workshop on Extracting and Using Constructions in Computational Linguistics, pages 1–8,
Los Angeles, California, June 2010.

translation, information retrieval, and text summarization. Consider, for instance, the following machine translation into Spanish by the Google translate (http://translate.google.com/):

They hissed him out of the university.
→ Silbaban fuera de la universidad.
Tr. They were whistling outside the university.[1]

The translation has absolutely no implication that a group of people did something to cause another person to leave the university. However, when the verb is changed to a verb that is seen to frequently appear in a caused motion interpretation (e.g. *throw*), the results are correct:

They threw him out of the university.
→ Lo sacaron de la universidad.
Tr. They took him out of the university.

Thus, if we could facilitate a caused motion interpretation by bootstrapping semantics from constructions (e.g. "X ___ Y *out of* Z" implies caused motion), we could enable accurate translations that otherwise would not be possible.

2 Current Approaches

In natural language processing (NLP), the issue of semantic analysis in the presence of lexical and syntactic variability is often perceived as the purview of either word sense disambiguation (WSD) or semantic role labeling (SRL) or both. In the case of WSD, the above issue is often tackled through the use of large corpora tagged with sense information to train a classifier to recognize the different shades of meaning of a semantically ambiguous word (Ng and Lee, 2006; Agirre and Edmonds, 2006). In the case of SRL, the goal is to identify each of the arguments of the predicate and label them according to their semantic relationship to the predicate (Gildea and Jurafsky, 2002).

There are several corpora available for training WSD classifiers such as WordNet's SemCor (Miller 1995; Fellbaum 1998) and the GALE OntoNotes data (Hovy et. al., 2006). However, most, if not all, of these corpora include only a small fraction of all English predicates. Since WSD systems train separate classifiers for each predicate, if a particular predicate does not exist in the sparse training data, a system cannot create an accurate semantic interpretation. Even if the predicate is present, the appropriate sense might not be. In such a case, the WSD will again be unable to contribute to a correct overall semantic interpretation. This is the case in example (1), where even the extremely fine-grained sense distinctions provided by WordNet do not include a sense of hiss that is consistent with the caused motion interpretation rendered in the example.

Available for SRL tasks are efforts such as PropBank (Palmer et al., 2005) and FrameNet (Fillmore et al., 2003) that have developed semantic role labels (based on differing approaches) and have labeled large corpora for training and testing of SRL systems. PropBank (PB) identifies and labels the semantic arguments of the verb on a verb-by-verb basis, creating a separate frameset that includes verb specific semantic roles to account for each subcategorization frame of the verb. Much like PB, FrameNet (FN) identifies and labels semantic roles, known as Frame Elements, around a relational target, usually a verb.[2] But unlike PB, Frame Elements less verb specific, but rather are defined in terms of semantic structures called *frames* evoked by the verb. That is, one or more verbs can be associated with a single semantic frame. Currently FN has over 2000 distinct Frame Elements.

The lexical resource VerbNet (Kipper-Schuler, 2005) details semantic classes of verbs, where a class is composed of verbs that have similar syntactic realizations, following work by Levin (1993). Verbs are grouped by their syntactic realization or *frames*, and each frame is associated with a meaning. For example, the verbs *loan* and *rent* are grouped together in class 13.1 with roughly a "give" meaning, and the verbs *deposit* and *situate* are grouped into 9.1 with roughly a "put" meaning.

Although differing in the nature of their tasks, WSD and SRL systems both treat lexical items as the source of meaning in a clause. In WSD, for every sense we need a new entry in our dictionary to be able to interpret the sentence. With SRL, we

[1] We have hand translated the Google translation back to English for comparison.

[2] PropBank labels Arg0 and Arg1, for the most part, correspond to Dowty's Prototypical Agent and Prototypical Patient, respectively, providing important generalizations.

need the semantic role labels that describe the predicate argument relationships in order to extract the meaning.

In either case, we are still left with the same issue – if the meaning lies in the lexical items, how do we interpret unseen words and novel lexical usages? As shown in the CoNLL-2005 shared task (Carreras and Marquez, 2005), system performance numbers drop significantly when a classifier, trained on the Wall Street Journal (WSJ) corpus, is tested on the Brown corpus. This is largely due to the "highly ambiguous and unseen predicates (i.e. predicates that do not have training examples)" (Giuglea and Moschitti, 2006).

3 Construction Grammar

This issue of scalability and generalizability across genres could possibly be improved by linking semantics more directly with syntax, as theorized by Construction Grammar (CxG) (Fillmore et. al., 1988; Golderg, 1995; Kay, 2002; Michaelis, 2004; Goldberg, 2006). This theory suggests that the meaning of a sentence arises not only from the lexical items but also from the patterned structures or *constructions* they sit in. The meaning of a given phrase, a sentence, or an utterance, then, arises from the combination of lexical items and the syntactic structure in which they are found, including any patterned structural configurations (e.g. patterns of idiomatic expressions such as "The Xer, the Yer" – *The bigger, the better*) or recurring structural elements (e.g. function words such as determiners, particles, conjunctions, and prepositions). That is, instead of focusing solely on the semantic label of words, as is done in SRL and in many traditional theories in Linguistics, CxG brings more into focus the interplay of lexical items and syntactic forms or structural patterns as the source of meaning.

3.1 Application of Construction Grammar

Thus, rather than just assigning labels at the level of lexical items and predicate arguments as a way of piecing together the meaning of a sentence, we follow the central premise of CxG. Specifically, that semantics *can be* and *should be* interpreted at the level of the larger structural configuration.

Consider the following three sentences, each having the same syntactic structure, each taken from different genres of writing available on the web.

Blogger arrested - blog him out of jail! [Blog]
Someone mind controlled me off the cliff. [Gaming]
He clocked the first pitch into center field. [Baseball]

Each of these sentences makes use of words, especially the verb, in ways particular to their genre. Even if we are unfamiliar with the specific jargon used, as a human we can infer the general meaning intended by each of the three sentences: *a person X causes an entity Y to move in the path specified by the prepositional phrase* (e.g. third sentence: "A player causes something to land in the center field.").

In a similar way, if we can assign a meaning of caused motion at the sentence level and an automatic learner can be trained to accurately identify the construction, then even when presented with an unseen word, a useful semantic analysis is still possible.

3.2 Caused-Motion Construction

For this effort, we focused on the *caused-motion construction*, which can be defined as having the coarse-grained syntactic structure of Subject Noun Phrase followed by a verb that takes both a Noun Phrase Object and a Prepositional Phrase: (NP-SBJ (V NP PP)); and the semantic meaning '*the agent, NP-SBJ, directly causes the patient, NP, to move along the path specified by the PP*' (Goldberg 1995). This construction is exemplified by the following sentences from (Goldberg 1995):

(2) Frank sneezed the tissue off the table.
(3) Mary urged Bill into the house.
(4) Fred stuffed the papers in the envelope.
(5) Sally threw a ball to him.

However, not all syntactic structures of the form (NP-SBJ (V NP PP)) belong to the caused-motion construction. Consider the following sentences.

(6) I considered Ben as one of my brothers.
(7) Jen took the highway into Pennsylvania.
(8) We saw the bird in the shopping mall.
(9) Mary kicked the ball to my relief.

In (6) and (9), the PPs do not specify a location, a direction or a path. In (8), the PP is a location;

however, the PP indicates the location in which the "seeing" event happened, not a path along which "we" caused "the bird" to move. Though the PP in (7) expresses a path, it is not a path in which Jen causes "the highway" to move.

3.3 Goals

As an initial step in determining the usefulness of construction grammar for interpreting semantics in computational linguistics, we present the results of our study aimed at ascertaining if a classifier can be taught to identify caused-motion constructions. We also report on our investigations into which features were most useful in the classification of caused-motion constructions.

4 Data & Experiments

The data for this study was pulled from the WSJ part of Penn Treebank II (Marcus et al., 1994). From this corpus, all sentences with the syntactic form (NP-SBJ (V NP PP)) were selected. The selection allowed for intervening adverbial phrases (e.g. *"Sally threw a ball quickly to him"*) and additional prepositional phrases (e.g. *"Sally threw a ball to him on Tuesday"* or *"Sally threw a ball in anger into the scorer's table"*). A total of 14.7k instances[3] were identified in this manner.

To reduce the size of the corpus to be labeled to a target of 1800 instances, we removed, firstly, instances containing traces as parsed by the TreeBank. These included passive usages (e.g. *"Coffee was shipped from Colombia by Gracie"*) and instances with traces in the object NP or PP including questions and relative clauses (e.g. *"What did Gracie ship from Colombia?")*. In construction grammar, however, traces do not exist, since grammar is a set of patterns of varying degrees of complexity. Thus CxG would characterize passives, questions structures, and relative clauses as having their own respective phrasal constructions, which combine with the caused-motion construction. In order to ensure sufficient training data with the standard form of the caused-motion construction as defined in Goldberg 1995 and 2006 (see Section 3.2), we chose to remove these usages.

Secondly, we removed the instances of sentences that can be deterministically categorized as non-caused motion constructions: instances containing ADV, EXT, PRD, VOC, or TMP type object NPs (e.g. *"Cindy drove **five hours** from Dallas"*, *"You listen, **boy**, to what I say!"*). Because we can automatically identify this category, keeping these examples in our data would have resulted in even higher performance.

We also considered the possibility of reducing the size by removing certain classes of verbs such as verbs of communication (e.g. *reply*, *bark*), psychological state (e.g. *amuse*, *admire*), or existence (e.g. *be*, *exist*). While it is reasonable to say that these verb types are highly unlikely to appear in a caused-motion construction, if we were to remove sets of verbs based on their likely behavior, we would also be excluding interesting usages such as *"The stand-up comedian amused me into a state of total enjoyment."* or *"The leader barked a command into a radio."*

After filtering these sentences, 8700 remained. From the remaining instances, we selected 1800 instances at random for the experiments presented.

4.1 Labels and Classifier

The 1800 instances were hand-labeled with one of the following two labels:

- Caused-Motion (CM)
- Non Caused-Motion (NON-CM)

The CM label included both literal usages (e.g. *"Well-wishers stuck little ANC flags in their hair."*) and non-literal usages (e.g. *"Producers shepherded 'Flashdance' through several scripts.")* of caused-motion.

After the annotation, the corpus was randomly divided into two sets: 75% for training data and 25% for testing data. The distribution of the labels in the test data is 33.3% CM and 66.7% NON-CM. The distribution in the training set is 31.8% CM and 68.2% NON-CM. For our experiments, we used a Support Vector Machine (SVM) classifier with a linear kernel. In particular we made use of the LIBSVM (Chang and Lin, 2001) as training and testing software.

[3] We use the term *instances* over *sentences* since a sentence can have more than one instance. For example, the sentence "I gave the ball to Bill, and he kicked it to the wall." is composed of 2 instances.

4.2 Baseline Features

The baseline consisted of a single conceptual feature - the lemmatized, case-normalized verb. We chose the verb as a baseline feature because it is generally accepted to be the core lexical item in a sentence, which governs the syntactic structure and semantic constituents around it. This is especially evidenced in the Penn Treebank where NP nodes are assigned with syntactic labels according to the position in the tree relative to the verb (e.g. Subject). In VerbNet and PropBank, the semantic labels are assigned to the constituents around the verb, each according to its semantic relationship with the verb.

This verb feature was encoded as 478 binary features (one for each unique verb in the dataset), where the feature value corresponding to the instance's verb was 1 and all others were 0.

4.3 Additional Features

In the present experiments, we utilize gold-standard values for two of the *PP features* for a proof of feasibility. Future work will evaluate the effect of automatically extracting these features. In addition to the baseline verb feature (feature 1), our full feature set consisted of 8 additional types for a total of 334 features. Examples used in the feature descriptions are pulled from our data.

PP features:

2. Preposition (76 features) The preposition heading the prepositional phrase (e.g. *"Producers shepherded 'Flashdance' [[**through**]$_P$ several scripts]$_{PP}$."*) was encoded as 76 binary features, one per preposition type in the training data. For instances with multiple PPs, preposition features were extracted from each of the PPs.
3. Function Tag on PP (11 features) Penn Treebank encodes grammatical, adverbial, and other related information on the PP's POS tag (e.g. "PP-LOC"). The function tag on the prepositional phrase was encoded as 10 binary features plus an extra feature for PPs without function tags. Again, for instances with multiple PPs, each corresponding function tag feature was set to 1.
4. Complement Category to P (19 features) Normally a PP node consists of a P and a NP. However, there are some cases where the complement of the P can be of a different syntactic category (e.g. *"So, view permanent insurance [[for]$_P$ [**what it is**]$_{SBAR}$]$_{PP}$."*). Thus, the phrasal category tags (e.g. NP, SBAR) of the preposition's sister nodes were encoded as 19 binary features. For instances with multiple PPs, all sister nodes of the prepositions were collected.

VerbNet features: The following features were automatically extracted from VerbNet classes with frames matching the target syntactic structure, namely "NP V NP PP".

5. VerbNet Classes (123 features) The verbs in the data were associated with one or more of the above VerbNet classes according to their membership. The VerbNet classes were then encoded as 122 binary features with one additional feature for verbs that were not found to be members of any of these classes. If a verb belongs to multiple matching classes, each corresponding feature was set.
6. VerbNet PP Type (27 features) VerbNet frames associate the PP with a description (e.g. "NP V NP PP.***location***"). The types were encoded as 26 binary features, plus an extra feature for PPs without a description. The features represented the union of all PP types (i.e. if a VerbNet class included multiple PPs, each of the corresponding features was assigned a value of 1). If a verb was associated with multiple VerbNet classes, the features were set according to the union over both the corresponding classes and their set of PP types.

Named Entity features: These features were automatically annotated using BBN's IdentiFinder (Bikel, 1999). The feature counts for the subject NP and object NP differ strictly due to what entities were represented in the data. For example, the entity type "DISEASE" was found in an object NP position but not in a subject NP.

7. NEs for Subject NP (23 features) The union of all named entities under the NP-SBJ node was encoded as 23 binary features.
8. NEs for Object NP (27 features) The union of all named entities under the object NP node was encoded as 27 binary features.
9. NEs for PP's Object (28 features) The union

of all named entities under the NP under the PP node was encoded as 28 binary features.

5 Results

For the baseline system, the model was built from the training data using a linear kernel and a cost parameter of C=1 (LIBSVM default value). When using the full feature set, the model was also built from the training data using a linear kernel, but the cost parameter was C=0.5, the best value from 10-fold cross validation on the training data.

In Table 1, we report the precision (P), recall (R), F_1 score, and accuracy (A) for identifying caused-motion constructions[4].

Features	P%	R%	F	A%
Baseline* Set	78.0	52.0	0.624	79.1
Full Set	87.2	86.0	0.866	91.1

Table 1: System Performance (*verb feature baseline)

The results show that the addition of the features presented in section 4.3 resulted in a significant increase in both precision and recall, which in turn boosted the F score from 0.624 to 0.857, an increase of 0.233.

6 Feature Performance

In order to determine the usefulness of the individual features in the classification of caused-motion, we evaluated the features in two ways. In one (Table 2), we compared the performance of each of the features to a majority class baseline (i.e. 66.7% accuracy). A useful feature was expected to show an increase over this baseline with statistical significance. Significance of each feature's performance was evaluated via a chi-squared test (p<0.05).

Our results show that the features 3, 1, 2 and 5 performed significantly better over the majority class baseline. The features 4, 7 and 8 were unable to distinguish between the caused-motion constructions and the non caused-motion usages.

[4] As we can see in Table 1, the accuracy is higher than precision or recall. This is because precision and recall are calculated with regard to identifying caused-motion constructions, whereas accuracy is based on identifying both caused-motion and non-caused motion constructions. Since it's easier to get better performance on the majority class (NON-CM), the overall accuracy is higher.

#	Included Feature	P%	R%	F	A%	
3	Preposition	82.4	65.3	0.729	83.8	*
1	Verb	78.0	52.0	0.624	79.1	*
2	Function Tag on PP	82.6	38.0	0.521	76.7	*
5	VerbNet Classes	73.5	33.3	0.459	73.8	*
6	VerbNet PP Type	59.6	33.3	0.427	70.2	
9	NEs for PP's Object	71.4	6.7	0.122	68.0	
4	Comp. Cat. of P		0.0		66.7	
7	NEs for Subject NP		0.0		66.7	
8	NEs for Object NP		0.0		66.7	

Table 2: Effect of each feature on the performance in classification of the caused-motion construction, in the order of decreasing F-score. Features that performed statistically higher than the majority class baseline are marked with an * in the last column.

Their precision values could not be calculated due to the fact that these features resulted in zero positive (CM) classification.

In a second study, we evaluated the performance of the system when each feature was removed individually from the full set of features (Table 3). The removal of a useful feature was expected to show a statistically significant drop in performance compared to that of the full feature set. Significance in this performance degradation when compared against the full set of features was evaluated via chi-squared test (p<0.05). Here, features 3, 8 and 1, when removed, showed a statistically significant performance drop. The rest of the features were not shown to have a statistically significant effect on the performance.

Our results show that the preposition feature is the single most predictive feature and the feature that has the most significant effect in the full feature set. These results are encouraging: unlike the purely lexical features like the named entity features (6, 7, and 8) that are dependent on the particular expression used in the sentence,

#	Removed Feature	P%	R%	F	A%	
3	Preposition	76.9	73.3	0.751	83.8	*
8	NEs for Object NP	84.6	80.7	0.826	88.7	*
1	Verb	85.9	81.3	0.836	89.3	*
2	Function Tag on PP	85.2	84.7	0.849	90.0	
9	NEs for PP's Object	87.5	84.0	0.857	90.7	
7	NEs for Subject NP	87.0	84.7	0.858	90.7	
5	VerbNet Classes	86.0	86.0	0.860	90.7	
4	Comp. Cat. of P	86.7	86.7	0.867	91.1	
6	VerbNet PP Type	87.8	86.0	0.869	91.3	

Table 3: System performance when the specified feature is removed from the full set of features, in the order of increasing F-score. Significant performance degradation, when compared against the full feature set performance (Table 1) was labeled with an * in the last column.

prepositions are function words. Like syntactic elements, these function words also contribute to the patterned structures of a construction as discussed in Section 3. Furthermore, unlike the semantics of features that are dependent on content words that are subject to lexical variability, prepositions are limited in their lexical variability, which make them good general features that scale well across different semantic domains.

In addition to the preposition feature, the verb feature was found to affect performance at a statistically significant level in both cases. Based on the numerous studies in the past that have shown the usefulness of the verb as a feature, this is not an unexpected result. Interestingly, our results seem to indicate interactions between features. This can be seen in two different instances. First, while feature 8 (NEs for Object NP) alone was not found to be a predictive feature, when removed, it resulted in a statistically significant drop in performance compared to that of the full feature set. The opposite effect can be seen with the VerbNet Classes feature. While it showed a statistically significant boost in performance when introduced into the system by itself, when dropped from the full feature set, the drop in the system performance was not found to be significant. This seems to indicate that NEs for Object NP and the VerbNet Classes features have strong interactions with one or more of the other features. We will continue investigating these interactions in future work.

7 Out-of-Vocabulary Verbs

Additionally, we separately examined the performance on the test set verbs that were not seen in the training data (i.e. out-of-vocabulary/OOV items). Just over a fifth of the instances (92 out of 450 constructions) in the test data had unseen verbs, with a total of 83 unique verb types. The results show that there was no decrease in the accuracy or F-score. In fact, there was a chance increase, not statistically significant, in a two-sample t-test ($t=1.13$; $p>0.2$).

We carried out the same feature studies for the OOV verbs, as detailed in section 6 (Tables 4 and 5). The performance in both of the studies reflected the results seen in Tables 2 and 3, with one expected exception. The verb feature was, of course, found to be of no value to the predictor.

#	Removed Feature	P%	R%	F	A%
3	Preposition	63	76	0.69	90
2	Function Tag on PP	83	80	0.82	82
6	VerbNet PP Type	84	84	0.84	67
5	VerbNet Classes	84	84	0.84	73
9	NEs for PP's Object	84	84	0.84	74
1	Verb		0		73
4	Comp. Cat. of P		0		73
7	NEs for Subject NP		0		73
8	NEs for Object NP		0		73

Table 4: Effect of each feature on the performance in classification of the caused-motion construction with OOV verbs, in the order of decreasing F-score. The precision values could not be calculated for the performance of the features 1,4,7, and 8 due to the fact that these features resulted in zero positive classifications.

What is interesting here is that the verb feature did perform at a significant level for the full test data. By this observation, it would be expected that the overall performance on the OOV verbs would be negatively affected since there is no available verb information. However, this was not the case.

8 Discussion and Conclusion

The results presented show that a classifier can be trained to automatically identify the semantics of constructions; at least for the caused-motion construction, and that it can do this with high accuracy. Furthermore, we have determined that the preposition feature is the most useful feature when identifying caused-motion constructions. Moreover, in considering our results in light of the performance of the SRL systems (Gildea and Jurafsky, 2002; Carreras and Marquez, 2005), where unseen predicates result in significant performance degradation, we found in contrast that using CxG to inform semantics resulted in equally high performance on the out-of-vocabulary predicates. This serves as evidence that semantic

#	Removed Feature	P%	R%	F	A%
3	Preposition	63	76	0.69	82
8	NEs for Object NP	83	80	0.82	90
2	Function Tag on PP	84	84	0.84	91
5	VerbNet Classes	84	84	0.84	91
7	NEs for Subject NP	84	84	0.84	91
1	Verb	88	88	0.88	93
4	Comp. Cat. of P	88	88	0.88	93
6	VerbNet PP Type	92	88	0.90	95
9	NEs for PP's Object	92	88	0.90	95

Table 5: System performance when the specified feature is removed from the full set of features in the classification of constructions with OOV items, in the order of increasing F-score.

analysis of novel lexical combinations and unseen verbs can be improved by enriching semantics with a construction-level analysis.

9 Future Work

There are several directions to go from here. First, in this paper we have kept our study within the scope of caused-motion constructions. We intend to introduce more types of constructions and include more syntactic variation in our data. We will also add more annotated instances. Secondly, we examine the impact of the introduction of additional features, such as a bag-of-words feature. In particular, we will include semantic features based on FrameNet to the VerbNet semantic features we are already using. This will be more feasible once the SemLink semantic role labeler for FrameNet becomes available (Palmer, 2009). Finally, we plan to include a more detailed analysis of the feature interactions, and examine the benefit that a construction grammar perspective might add to our semantic analysis.

Acknowledgements

We gratefully acknowledge the support of the Defense Advanced Research Projects Agency (DARPA/IPTO) under the GALE program, DARPA/CMO Contract No. HR0011-06-C-0022, subcontract from BBN, Inc. We are also grateful to Laura Michaelis for helpful discussions and comments.

References

Agirre, Eneko and Philip Edmonds. 2006. Introduction. In Word Sense Disambiguation: Algorithms and Applications, Agirre and Edmonds (eds.), Springer.

Ben-David, Shai, Blitzer, John, Crammer, Koby Pereira, Fernando. 2006. 'Analysis of representations for domain adaptation', in *NIPS.*

Bikel, D., Schwartz, R., Weischedel, R. 1999. An algorithm that learns what's in a name. Machine Learning: Special Issue on NL Learning, 34, 1-3.

Carreras, Xavier and Lluis Marquez. 2005. Introduction to the CoNLL- 2005 shared task: Semantic role labeling. Procs of CoNLL- 2005.

Chih-Chung Chang and Chih-Jen Lin, LIBSVM : a library for support vector machines, 2001. Software available at http://www.csie.ntu.edu.tw/~cjlin/libsvm

Gildea, Daniel and Daniel Jurafsky. 2002. Automatic Labeling of Semantic Roles. Computational Linguistics 28:3, 245-288.

Fillmore, Charles J., Christopher R. Johnson and Miriam R.L. Petruck (2003) Background to Framenet, International Journal of Lexicography, Vol 16.3: 235-250.

Fillmore, Charles, Paul Kay and Catherine O'Connor (1988). Regularity and Idiomaticity in Grammatical Constructions: The Case of *let alone. Language* 64: 501-38.

Giuglea, Ana-Maria and Alessandro Moschitti. 2006. Shallow semantic parsing based on FrameNet, Verb-Net and PropBank. In Proceedings of the 17th European Conference on Artificial Intelligence, Riva del Garda, Italy.

Goldberg, Adele E. 2006. Constructions at work. The nature of generalization in language. Oxford: Oxford University Press

Goldberg, Adele. E. 1995. Constructions: A construction grammar approach to argument structure. Chicago: University of Chicago Press.

Hovy, Edward H., Mitch Marcus, Martha Palmer, Sameer Pradhan, Lance Ramshaw, and Ralph M. Weischedel. 2006. OntoNotes: The 90% Solution. Short paper. Proceedings of the Human Language Technology / North American Association of Computational Linguistics conference (HLT-NAACL 2006). pp. 57-60, New York, NY.

Kay, Paul. 2002. English Subjectless Tag Sentences. Language 78: 453-81.

Kipper-Schuler, Karin. 2005. VerbNet: A broad coverage, comprehensive verb lexicon. Ph.D. thesis, University of Pennsylvania.

Levin, Beth. 1993. English Verb Classes and Alternations: A Preliminary Investigation, University of Chicago Press, Chicago, IL.

Michaelis, Laura A. (2004). Type Shifting in Construction Grammar: An Integrated Approach to Aspectual Coercion. *Cognitive Linguistics* 15: 1-67.

Ng, Hwee Tou and Hian Beng Lee. 1996. Integrating multiple knowledge sources to disambiguate word sense: An exemplar-based approach. Proceedings of the 34th Annual Meeting of the Association for Computational Linguistics, Santa Cruz, California, 40–47.

Marcus, Mitchell P, Santorini, Beatrice, Marcinkiewicz, Mary A. (1994) "Building a large annotated corpus of English: the Penn Treebank" Computational Linguistics 19: 313-330.

Palmer, Martha. "Semlink: Linking PropBank, VerbNet and FrameNet." Proceedings of the Generative Lexicon Conference. Sept. 2009, Pisa, Italy: GenLex-09, 2009.

Palmer, Martha, Daniel Gildea, and Paul Kingsbury. 2005. The Proposition Bank: An Annotated Corpus of Semantic Roles. Computational Linguistics, 31(1):71–106.

Towards an Inventory of English Verb Argument Constructions

Matthew Brook O'Donnell
University of Michigan
500 E. Washington St.
Ann Arbor, MI 48104, USA
mbod@umich.edu

Nick Ellis
University of Michigan
500 E. Washington St.
Ann Arbor, MI 48104, USA
ncellis@umich.edu

Abstract

This paper outlines and pilots our approach towards developing an inventory of verb-argument constructions based upon English form, function, and usage. We search a tagged and dependency-parsed BNC (a 100-million word corpus of English) for Verb-Argument Constructions (VACs) including those previously identified in the pattern grammar resulting from the COBUILD project. This generates (1) a list of verb types that occupy each construction. We next tally the frequency profiles of these verbs to produce (2) a frequency ranked type-token distribution for these verbs, and we determine the degree to which this is Zipfian. Since some verbs are faithful to one construction while others are more promiscuous, we next produce (3) a contingency-weighted list reflecting their statistical association. To test whether each of these measures is a step towards increasing the learnability of VACs as categories, following principles of associative learning, we examine 20 verbs from each distribution. Here we explore whether there is an increase in the semantic cohesion of the verbs occupying each construction using semantic similarity measures. From inspection, this seems to be so. We are developing measures of this using network measures of clustering in the verb-space defined by WordNet and Roget's Thesaurus.

1 Construction grammar and Usage

Constructions are form-meaning mappings, conventionalized in the speech community, and entrenched as language knowledge in the learner's mind. They are the symbolic units of language relating the defining properties of their morphological, lexical, and syntactic form with particular semantic, pragmatic, and discourse functions (Goldberg, 2006). Construction Grammar argues that all grammatical phenomena can be understood as learned pairings of form (from morphemes, words, idioms, to partially lexically filled and fully general phrasal patterns) and their associated semantic or discourse functions: "the network of constructions captures our grammatical knowledge *in toto*, i.e. It's constructions all the way down" (Goldberg, 2006, p. 18). Such beliefs, increasingly influential in the study of child language acquisition, have turned upside down generative assumptions of innate language acquisition devices, the continuity hypothesis, and top-down, rule-governed, processing, bringing back data-driven, emergent accounts of linguistic systematicities.

Frequency, learning, and language come together in usage-based approaches which hold that we learn linguistic constructions while engaging in communication. The last 50 years of psycholinguistic research provides the evidence of usage-based acquisition in its demonstrations that language processing is exquisitely sensitive to usage frequency at all levels of language representation from phonology, through lexis and syntax, to sentence processing (Ellis, 2002). Language knowledge involves statistical knowledge, so humans learn more easily and process more fluently high frequency forms and 'regular' patterns which are exemplified by many types and which have few competitors. Psycholinguistic perspectives thus hold that language learning is the associative learning of representations that reflect the probabilities of occurrence of form-function mappings. Frequency is a key determinant of acquisition because 'rules' of language, at all levels of analysis from phonology, through syntax, to discourse, are structural regularities which emerge from learners' lifetime unconscious analysis of the distributional characteristics of the language input.

If constructions as form-function mappings are the units of language, then language acquisition involves inducing these associations from experience of language usage. Constructionist accounts of language acquisition thus involve the distributional analysis of the language stream and the parallel analysis of contingent perceptuo-motor activ-

Proceedings of the NAACL HLT Workshop on Extracting and Using Constructions in Computational Linguistics, pages 9–16,
Los Angeles, California, June 2010.

ity, with abstract constructions being learned as categories from the conspiracy of concrete exemplars of usage following statistical learning mechanisms (Bod, Hay, & Jannedy, 2003; Bybee & Hopper, 2001; Ellis, 2002) relating input and learner cognition. Psychological analyses of the learning of constructions as form-meaning pairs is informed by the literature on the associative learning of cue-outcome contingencies where the usual determinants include: (1) input frequency (type-token frequency, Zipfian distribution, recency), (2) form (salience and perception), (3) function (prototypicality of meaning, importance of form for message comprehension, redundancy), and (4) interactions between these (contingency of form-function mapping) (Ellis & Cadierno, 2009).

2 Determinants of construction learning

In natural language, Zipf's law (Zipf, 1935) describes how a handful of the highest frequency words account for the most linguistic tokens. Zipf's law states that the frequency of words decreases as a power function of their rank in the frequency table. If p_f is the proportion of words whose frequency rank in a given language sample is *f*, then $p_f \sim f^{-b}$, with $b \approx 1$. Zipf showed this scaling relation holds across a wide variety of language samples. Subsequent research provides support for this law as a linguistic universal: many language events (e.g., frequencies of phoneme and letter strings, of words, of grammatical constructs, of formulaic phrases, etc.) across scales of analysis follow this law (Solé, Murtra, Valverde, & Steels, 2005).

Goldberg, Casenhiser & Sethuraman (2004) demonstrated that in samples of child language acquisition, for a variety of verb-argument constructions (VACs), there is a strong tendency for one single verb to occur with very high frequency in comparison to other verbs used, a profile which closely mirrors that of the mothers' speech to these children. Goldberg et al. (2004) show that Zipf's law applies within VACs too, and they argue that this promotes acquisition: tokens of one particular verb account for the lion's share of instances of each particular argument frame; this pathbreaking verb also is the one with the prototypical meaning from which the construction is derived (see also Ninio, 1999).

Ellis and Ferreira-Junior (2009) investigate effects upon naturalistic second language acquisition of type/token distributions in three English verb-argument constructions. They show that VAC verb type/token distribution in the input is Zipfian and that learners first acquire the most frequent, prototypical and generic exemplar. (e.g. *put* in VOL [verb-object-locative], *give* in VOO [verb-object-object], etc.). Acquisition is affected by the frequency distribution of exemplars within each island of the construction, by their prototypicality, and, using a variety of psychological (Shanks, 1995) and corpus linguistic association metrics (Gries & Stefanowitsch, 2004), by their contingency of form-function mapping. This fundamental claim that Zipfian distributional properties of language usage helps to make language learnable has thus begun to be explored for these three VACs, at least. It remains an important research agenda to explore its generality across a wide range of constructions (i.e. the constructicon).

The primary motivation of construction grammar is that we must bring together linguistic form, learner cognition, and usage. An important consequence is that constructions cannot be defined purely on the basis of linguistic form, *or* semantics, *or* frequency of usage *alone*. All three factors are necessary in their operationalization and measurement. Our research aims to do this. We hope to describe the verbal grammar of English, to analyze the way VACs map form and meaning, and to provide an inventory of the verbs that exemplify constructions and their frequency. This last step is necessary because the type-token frequency distribution of their verbs determines VAC acquisition as abstract schematic constructions, and because usage frequency determines their entrenchment and processing.

This paper describes and pilots our approach. We focus on just two constructions for illustration here (V *across* n, and V Obj Obj) although our procedures are principled, generic and applicable to all VACs. We search a tagged and dependency-parsed British National Corpus (a 100-million word corpus of English) for VACs including those previously identified in the COBUILD pattern grammar project. This generates (1) a list of verb types that occupy each construction. We next tally the frequency profiles of these verbs to produce (2) a frequency ranked type-token distribution for these verbs, and we determine the degree to which this is Zipfian. Since some verbs are faithful to one construction while others are more promiscuous, we next produce (3) a contingency-weighted list which reflects their statistical association.

3 Method

As a starting point, we considered several of the major theories and datasets of construction grammar such as FrameNet (Fillmore, Johnson, & Petruck, 2003). However, because our research aims to empirically determine the semantic associations of particular linguistic forms, it is important that such forms are initially defined by bottom-up means that are semantics-free. There is no one in corpus linguistics who 'trusts the text' more than Sinclair (2004). Therefore we chose the Pattern Grammar (Francis et al. 1996) definition of Verb constructions that arose out of his Cobuild project.

3.1 Construction inventory: COBUILD Verb Patterns

The form-based patterns described in the COBUILD Verb Patterns volume (Francis et al. 1996) take the form of word class and lexis combinations, such as V *across* n, V *into* n and *V n n*. For each of these patterns the resource provides information as to the structural configurations and functional/meaning groups found around these patterns through detailed concordance analysis of the Bank of English corpus during the construction of the COBUILD dictionary. For instance, the following is provided for the V *across* n pattern (Francis, et al., 1996, p. 150):

> The verb is followed by a prepositional phrase which consists of across and a noun group.
>
> This pattern has one structure:
> * Verb with Adjunct.
> *I cut across the field.*

Further example sentences are provided drawn from the corpus and a list of verbs found in the pattern and that are semantically typical are given. For this pattern these are: *brush, cut, fall, flicker, flit plane, skim, sweep*. No indication is given as to how frequent each of these types are or how comprehensive the list is. Further structural (syntactical) characteristics of the pattern are sometimes provided, such as the fact that for V *across* n the prepositional phrase is an adjunct and that the verb is never passive.

For some construction patterns with a generally fixed order it may be sufficient just to specify combinations of word and part-of-speech sequences. For example, a main verb followed by *across* within 1 to 3 words (to allow for adverbial elements), followed by a noun or pronoun within a few words. To such constraints a number exceptions of what should not occur within the specified spans must be added. The variation and potential complexity of English noun phrases presents challenges for this approach. On the other hand a multi-level constituent parse tree provides more than needed. A dependency parse with word-to-word relations is well suited for the task.

3.2 Corpus: BNC XML Parsed

The analysis of verb type-token distribution in the kinds of construction patterns described in the previous section should ideally be carried out using a range of corpora in the magnitude of the tens or hundreds of millions of words as the original work is derived from the Bank of English (a growing monitor corpus of over 400 million words). These corpora should, at the least, be part-of-speech tagged to search for the pattern as specified. Further some kind of partial parsing and chunking is necessary to apply the structural constraints (see Mason & Hunston, 2004 for exploratory methodology). We chose to use the 100 million word British National Corpus (BNC) on account of its size, the breadth of genres it contains and consistent lemmatization and part-of-speech tagging. Andersen et al. (2008) parsed the XML version of the BNC using the RASP parser (Briscoe, Carroll, & Watson, 2006). RASP is a statistical feature-based parser that produces a probabilistically ordered set of parse trees for a given sentence and additionally a set of grammatical relations (GRs) that capture "those aspects of predicate-argument structure that the system is able to recover and is the most stable and grammar independent representation available" (Briscoe, et al., 2006, p. 79). The GRs are organized into a hierarchy of dependency relations, including distinctions between modifiers and arguments and within arguments between subject (sub) and complements (comp). Figure 1 shows the GRs assigned by RASP for the sentence: *The kitchen light skids across the lawn* (BNC A0U). The main verb *skids* has two arguments, a subject (ncsubj) and indirect object (iobj), and the preposition one argument (dobj).

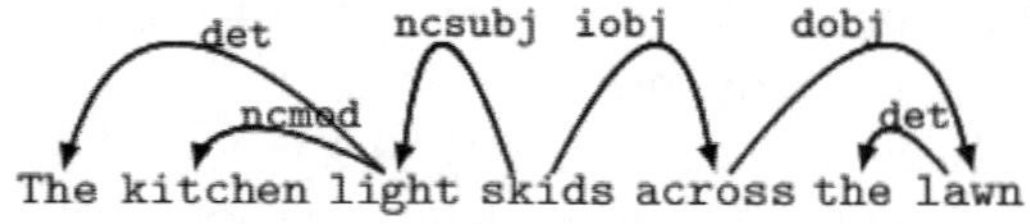

Figure 1. Example of RASP GRs

The RASP GR hierarchy does not include categories such as prepositional complement or adjunct. Figure 2 shows the GRs for another sentence containing *across* which is not an example of the V *across* n pattern. Alternate analyses might attach *across* directly to the main verb *threw*, but at least from examining BNC examples containing *across*, it appears RASP tends to favor local attachments (also for *towards* in this case).

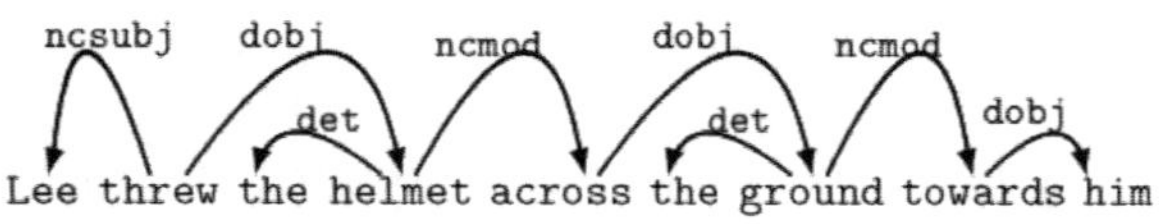

Figure 2. Example of RASP GRs

The GRs from RASP have been incorporated into the XML for each BNC sentence thereby preserving the token, part-of-speech and lemma information in the corpus.

3.3 Searching construction patterns

Our search algorithm works as follows:

1. Process each sentence in turn testing against an XPath expression to identify components in construction patterns, e.g. `.//w[@lem="across"][@pos="PREP"]/preceding-sibling::w[position()<3][@pos="VERB"][1]` finds a verb followed by *across* within 2 words.
2. Create a list of the grammatical relations where this verb functions as the head.
   i. This finds the `ncsubj` and `iobj` relations for the example sentence.
   ii. Also find GRs involving other components of pattern (e.g. *across*).
3. Check these GRs against a constraint list, e.g. make sure that
   i. only one relation where the dependent word comes after the verb (excluding verbs with both `dobj` and `iobj` or `obj2`)
   ii. the dependent of the second component matches a specific part-of-speech (e.g. *across* as head and noun as dependent).
4. For matching sentences record verb lemma.

Here we report on just two construction patterns: 1. V *across* n and 2. V n n or V Obj Obj (where n includes both nouns and pronouns). We have also run a range of similar V Prep n patterns from COBUILD, such as V *into* n, V *after* n, V *as* n. We have still to carry out a systematic precision-recall analysis, but ad hoc examination suggests that the strict constraints using the dependency relations provides a reasonable precision and the size of the corpus results in a large enough number of tokens to carry out distributional analysis (see Table 1).

Construction	Types	Tokens	TTR
V *across* n	799	4889	16.34
V Obj Obj	663	9183	7.22

Table 1. Type-Token data for V *across* n and V Obj Obj constructions

3.4 Identifying the meaning of verb types occupying the constructions

We considered several ways of analyzing the semantics the resulting verb distributions. It is important that the semantic measures we employ are defined in a way that is free of linguistic distributional information, otherwise we would be building in circularity. Therefore methods such as LSA are not applicable here. Instead, our research utilizes two distribution-free semantic databases: (1) Roget's thesaurus, a classic lexical resource of long-standing proven utility, based on Roget's guided introspections, as implemented in the Open Roget's Project (Kennedy, 2009). This provides various algorithms for measuring the semantic similarity between terms and between sentences. (2) WordNet, based upon psycholinguistic theory and in development since 1985 (Miller, 2009). WordNet classes words into a hierarchical network. At the top level, the hierarchy for verbs is organized into 15 base types (such as *move1* expressing translational movement and *move2* movement without displacement, *communicate*, etc.) which then split into over 11,500 verb synonym sets or synsets.

Verbs are linked in the hierarchy according to relations such as hypernym (to *move* is an hypernym of to *walk*), and troponym, the term used for hyponymic relations in the verb component of WordNet (to *lisp* is a troponym of to *talk*). There are various algorithms to determine the semantic similarity between synsets in WordNet which consider the distance between the conceptual categories of words, as well as considering the hierarchical structure of the WordNet (Pedersen et al. 2004).

3.5 Determining the contingency between construction form and function

Some verbs are closely tied to a particular construction (for example, *give* is highly indicative of the ditransitive construction, whereas *leave*, although it can form a ditransitive, is more often associated with other constructions such as the simple transitive or intransitive). The more reliable the contingency between a cue and an outcome, the more readily an association between them can be learned (Shanks, 1995), so constructions with more faithful verb members are more transparent and thus should be more readily acquired. Ellis and Ferreira-Junior (2009) use ΔP and collostructional analysis measures (Stefanowitsch & Gries, 2003) to show effects of form-function contingency upon L2 VAC acquisition. Others use conditional probabilities to investigate contingency effects in VAC acquisition. This is still an active area of inquiry, and more research is required before we know which statistical measures of form-function contingency are more predictive of acquisition and processing. Meanwhile, the simplest usable measure is one of faithfulness – the proportion of tokens of total verb usage as a whole that appear in this particular construction. For illustration, the faithfulness of *give* to the ditransitive is approximately 0.40; that for *leave* is 0.01.

4 Results

4.1 Evaluating the verb distribution

For the V *across* n pattern the procedure outlined in the previous section results in the following list:

come	483					
walk	203 .					
cut	199	veer	4			
run	175	whirl	4	...		
spread	146	slice	4	discharge	1	
...		clamber	4	navigate	1	
		.		scythe	1	
				scroll	1	

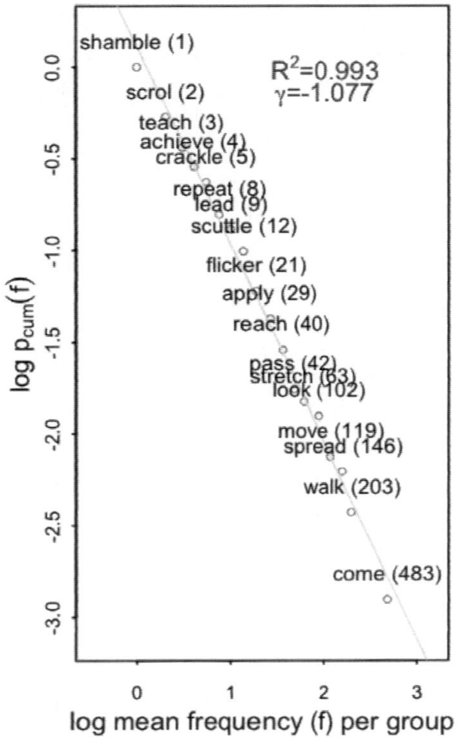

Figure 3. Verb type distribution for V *across* n

At first glance this distribution does appear to be Zipfian, exhibiting the characteristic long-tailed distribution in a plot of rank against frequency. Dorogovstev & Mendes (2003, pp. 222-223) outline the commonly used methods for measuring power-law distributions: 1. a simple log-log plot (rank/frequency), 2. log-log plot of cumulative probability against frequency and 3. the use of logarithmic binning over the distribution for a log-log plot as in 2. Linear regression can be applied to the resulting plots and goodness of fit (R^2) and the slope (γ) recorded.

Figure 3 shows such a plot for verb type frequency of the V *across* n construction pattern extracted from the parsed BNC XML corpus following the third plotting method. Verb types are grouped into 20 logarithmic bins according to their frequency (x-axis) against the logarithm of the cumulative probability of a verb occurring with or above this frequency (y-axis). Each point represents one bin and a verb from each group is randomly selected to label the point with its token frequency in parentheses. For example, the type *look* occurs 102 times in the V *across* n pattern and is placed into the 15th bin with the types *go*, *lie* and *lean*. Points towards the lower right of the plot indicate high-frequency low-type groupings and those towards the top left low-frequency high-type groupings, that is the fat- or long-tail of the distribution. Looking at the verbs given as examples of the pattern in COBUILD volume we find all but *plane* represented in our corpus search V *across* n: *brush* (12 tokens, group 9), *cut* (199 tokens, group 18), *fall* (57, g14), *flicker* (21, g10), *flit* (15, g9), *plane* (0), *skim* (9, g8), *sweep* (34, g12).

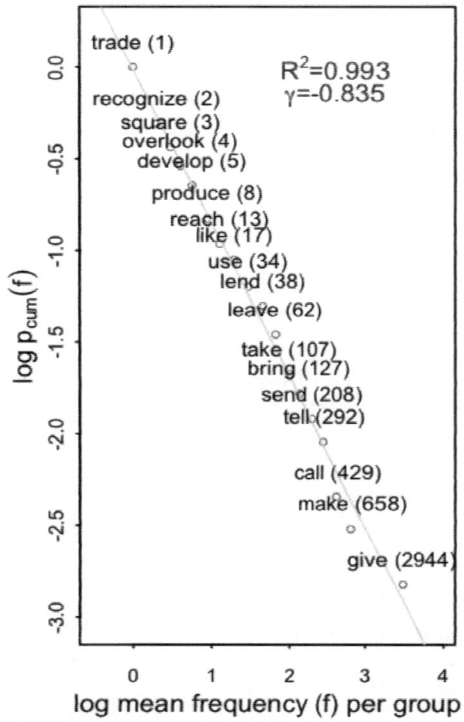

Figure 4. Verb type distribution for V Obj Obj

Figure 4 shows the plot for verb type frequency of the ditransitive V Obj Obj construction pattern extracted and binned in the same way. Both distributions can be fitted with a straight regression line (R^2=0.993). Thus we conclude that the type-token frequency distributions for these constructions are Zipfian. (In future we will investigate the other plot and fitting methods to ensure we have not smoothed the data too much through binning.) Inspection of the construction verb types, from most frequent down, also suggests that, as in prior research (Ellis & Ferreira-Junior, 2009; Goldberg et al., 2004; Ninio, 1999), the most frequent items are prototypical of the construction and more generic in their action semantics.

4.2 Evaluating the roles of frequency distribution and faithfulness in semantic cohesion

The second step in evaluating the verb distributions from the construction patterns is to compare a small set of types selected on the basis of a flat type distribution, the (Zipfian) token frequency distribution and a distribution that represents the degree to which a verb is attracted to the particular construction. First we select the top 200 types from the two VACs, ordered by token frequency. Then we sample 20 verbs from this list at random. This is the 'types list'. Next we take the top 20 types as the 'tokens list'. Finally, we calculate the tokenized faithfulness score for each type by dividing the verb's frequency in the construction by its overall frequency in the whole BNC. For example, *spread* occurs 146 times in the V *across* n pattern and 5503 times in total. So its faithfulness is 146/5503*100 = 2.65%, i.e. 1 in 38, of the instances of *spread* occur as *spread across* n. The tokenized faithfulness score for *spread* is then simply (146/5503) * 146 = 3.87, which tempers the tendency for low frequency types such as *scud*, *skitter* and *emblazon* to rise to the top of the list and is our initial attempt to combine the effects of token frequency and construction contingency. We reorder the 200 types by this figure and take the top twenty for the 'faithfulness list'. Tables 2 and 3 contain these lists for the two constructions. An intuitive reading of these lists suggests that the tokens list captures the most general and prototypical senses (*walk, move* etc. for V *across* n and *give, make, tell, offer* for V Obj Obj), while the list ordered by tokenized faith highlights some quite construction specific (and low frequency) items, such as *scud*, *flit* and *flicker* for V *across* n.

The final component is to quantify the semantic coherence or 'clumpiness' of the verbs extracted in the previous steps. For this we use WordNet and Roget's. Pedersen et al. (2004) outline six measures in their Perl WordNet::Similarity package, three (*path, lch* and *wup*) based on the path length between concepts in WordNet Synsets and three (*res, jcn* and *lin*) that incorporate a measure called 'information content' related to concept specificity. Tables 4 and 5 show the similarity scores that result from taking the 20 types in each of the lists in Tables 2 and 3 and generating a 20 by 20 distance matrix.

	types (sample)	**tokens**	**faithfulness**
1	scuttle	come	spread
2	ride	walk	scud
3	paddle	cut	sprawl
4	communicate	run	cut
5	rise	spread	walk
6	stare	move	come
7	drift	look	stride
8	stride	go	lean
9	face	lie	flit
10	dart	lean	stretch
11	flee	stretch	run
12	skid	fall	scatter
13	print	get	skitter
14	shout	pass	flicker
15	use	reach	slant
16	stamp	travel	scuttle
17	look	fly	stumble
18	splash	stride	sling
19	conduct	scatter	skid
20	scud	sweep	flash

Table 2. Top 20 types for V *across* n ordered by types, tokens and construction tokenized faithfulness

	types (sample)	**tokens**	**faithfulness**
1	eat	give	give
2	attend	make	call
3	feel	call	offer
4	receive	tell	make
5	miss	do	send
6	choose	offer	tell
7	affect	send	hand
8	come	show	show
9	mean	find	earn
10	provide	get	owe
11	cut	bring	cost
12	strike	ask	lend
13	prove	take	bring
14	teach	pay	do
15	refuse	allow	find
16	spare	buy	ask
17	leave	see	pay
18	wonder	hand	allow
19	permit	cost	buy
20	force	set	teach

Table 3. Top 20 types for V Obj Obj ordered by types, tokens and construction faithfulness

The figures are the mean of the values in each matrix. *Path* and *lin* values range between 0 and 1, Open Roget between 4 and 16 and the others are on varying scales where larger values indicate greater similarity. These tables show that the token distribution sample of verb types increases the semantic cohesion of the construction over a flat verbs list.

Similarity measure	Types (sampled)	Tokens (top 20)	Faithfulness (top 20)
WordNet			
path	0.163	0.387	0.245
lch	0.941	1.976	1.385
wup	0.312	0.653	0.453
res	2.473	4.673	3.748
jcn	1.033	0.383	0.190
lin	0.259	0.583	0.372
Open Roget	5.190	11.737	6.232

Table 4. Semantic similarity measures for V *across* n by types, tokens and construction faithfulness

Similarity measure	Types (sampled)	Tokens (top 20)	Faithfulness (top 20)
WordNet			
path	0.175	0.316	0.241
lch	1.008	1.654	1.299
wup	0.345	0.579	0.457
res	2.470	3.942	2.973
jcn	0.199	0.435	0.313
lin	0.308	0.558	0.406
Open Roget	7.863	13.011	10.768

Table 5. Semantic similarity measures for V Obj Obj by types, tokens and construction faithfulness

Sampling the items on the basis of their token frequency weighted for faithfulness also improves semantic homogeneity, although it does not here offer any improvement over a tokenized distribution alone. We not entirely satisfied with these measures. WordNet verb hierarchies are much flatter and bushier than those for nouns, where these measures are more successful. For verbs, distance down a synset is less telling than distance across. As a result, we are exploring other measures of the semantic similarity of verbs informed by network science. We are also exploring the use of word sense disambiguation techniques to reduce problems introduced by the rich polysemy of verbs in WordNet (e.g. *give* is assigned to 44 different synsets) and also in Roget's.

Future work

We plan to apply these methods to the full range of English VACs as described in Francis *et al* (1996)

and other construction grammars too. We are particularly interested in whether the inventory represents an optimal partitioning of verb semantics, starting with basic categories of action semantics and proceeding to greater specificity via Zipfian mapping. We are also interested in extending these approaches to learner language to investigate whether first and second language learners' acquisition follows the construction distributional profiles and whether the factors outlined in Goldberg et al. (2004) facilitate acquisition.

There have been suggestions that Zipfian type-token frequency distributions are essentially uninteresting artifacts. For each motivated construction identified along the lines described in 3.3, we have begun to make matching random control distributions generated as a random selection of verb types of comparable *n* types and tokens (yoked ersatz-controls). For each of our outcome measures, we will compare the various scores for VAC verb-types gathered on the principled basis of construction-grammar against those for their controls.

Conclusions

Meanwhile, these pilot studies show some promise in these methods towards an English verb grammar operationalized as an inventory of VACs, their verb membership and their type-token frequency distributions, their contingency of mapping, and their semantic motivations.

References

Andersen, Ø. E., Nioche, J., Briscoe, T., & Carroll, J. (2008). The BNC Parsed with RASP4UIMA. *Proceedings of the Sixth International Language Resources and Evaluation (LREC08)*, 28-30.

Bod, R., Hay, J., & Jannedy, S. (eds.). (2003). *Probabilistic linguistics*. Cambridge,MA: MIT Press.

Briscoe, E., Carroll, J., & Watson, R. (2006). *The Second Release of the RASP System.* Proceedings of the COLING/ACL 2006 Interactive Presentation Sessions, Sydney, Australia.

Bybee, J., & Hopper, P. (Eds.). (2001). *Frequency and the emergence of linguistic structure*. Amsterdam: Benjamins.

Dorogovstev, S.N., & Mendes, J.F.F. (2003). *Evolution of Networks: From Biological Nets to the Internet and WWW*. Oxford: Oxford University Press.

Ellis, N.C. (2002). Frequency effects in language processing: A review with implications for theories of implicit and explicit language acquisition. *Studies in Second Language Acquisition, 24* (2), 143-188.

Ellis, N.C., & Cadierno, T. (2009). Constructing a second language. *Annual Review of Cognitive Linguistics, 7* (Special section).

Ellis, N.C., & Ferreira-Junior, F. (2009). Constructions and their acquisition: Islands and the distinctiveness of their occupancy. *Annual Review of Cognitive Linguistics*, 111-139.

Fillmore, C. J., Johnson, C. R., & Petruck, M. R. L. (2003). Background to Framenet. *International Journal of Lexicography, 16*, 235-250.

Francis, G., Hunston, S., & Manning, E. (Eds.). (1996). *Grammar Patterns 1: Verbs. The COBUILD Series*. London: Harper Collins.

Goldberg, A.E. (2006). *Constructions at work: The nature of generalization in language*. Oxford: Oxford University Press.

Goldberg, A.E., Casenhiser, D.M., & Sethuraman, N. (2004). Learning argument structure generalizations. *Cognitive Linguistics,* 15, 289–316.

Gries, S.T., & Stefanowitsch, A. (2004). Extending collostructional analysis: a corpus-based perspective on 'alternations'. *International Journal of Corpus Linguistics, 9*, 97-129.

Kennedy, A. (2009). The Open Roget's Project: Electronic lexical knowledge base. Retr. 1st March, 2010: http://rogets.site.uottawa.ca/index.shtml

Mason, O., & Hunston, S. (2004). The automatic recognition of verb patterns: A feasibility study. *International Journal of Corpus Linguistics, 9*, 253-270.

Miller, G. A. (2009). WordNet - About us. Retrieved March 1, 2010, from http://wordnet.princeton.edu

Ninio, A. (1999). Pathbreaking verbs in syntactic development and the question of prototypical transitivity. *Journal of Child Language, 26*, 619-653.

Pedersen, T., Patwardhan, S., & Michelizzi, J. (2004). *WordNet::Similarity – Measuring the Relatedness of Concepts.* Proceedings of Fifth Annual Meeting of the North American Chapter of the Association of Computational Linguistics (NAACL 2004).

Shanks, D. R. (1995). *The psychology of associative learning*. New York: Cambridge University Press.

Sinclair, J. (2004). *Trust the text: Language, corpus and discourse*. London: Routledge.

Solé, R. V., Murtra, B., Valverde, S., & Steels, L. (2005). Language Networks: their structure, function and evolution. *Trends in Cognitive Sciences, 12*.

Stefanowitsch, A., & Gries, S.T. (2003). Collostructions: Investigating the interaction between words and constructions. *International Journal of Corpus Linguistics, 8*, 209-243.

Zipf, G. K. (1935). *The psycho-biology of language: An introduction to dynamic philology*. Cambridge, MA: The M.I.T. Press.

Identifying Assertions in Text and Discourse: The Presentational Relative Clause Construction

Cecily Jill Duffield, Jena D. Hwang, and Laura A. Michaelis
Department of Linguistics, Institute of Cognitive Science
University of Colorado at Boulder
Boulder, CO 80309 USA
{cecily.duffield, hwangd, laura.michaelis}@colorado.edu

Abstract

In this paper we investigate the Presentational Relative Clause (PRC) construction. In both the linguistic and NLP literature, relative clauses have been considered to contain background information that is not directly relevant or highly useful in semantic analysis. In text summarization in particular, the information contained in the relative clauses is often removed, being viewed as non-central content to the topic or discourse. We discuss the importance of distinguishing the PRC construction from other relative clause types. We show that in the PRC, the relative clause, rather than the main clause, contains the assertion of the utterance. Based on linguistic analysis, we suggest informative features that may be used in automatic extraction of PRC constructions. We believe that identifying this construction will be useful in discriminating central information from peripheral.

1 Introduction

Identifying and extracting relevant information in a given text is an important task for human readers and natural language processing applications. To do this, proper identification and treatment of complex sentences containing relative clauses and other embedded structures such as appositive clauses (e.g., *My mother, **a patient at the center,** met him last year,*) and participial clauses (e.g., *Once he ate Werthers, **including the wrapper,***) is necessary.

Thus, the tasks of text simplification and text summarization in NLP have focused their efforts on finding effective ways of simplifying long and complex sentences into shorter and simpler ones. This has in turn proven useful in machine translation (Chandrasekar et. al., 1996), parsing and information extraction (Chandrasekar and Srinivas, 1997), as well as document simplification designed to make texts accessible to wider audiences. Such audiences include readers at low literacy levels (Siddharthan, 2003), second language learners (Petersen and Ostendorf, 2007) and aphasic readers (Devilin and Unthank, 2006).

The goal of text simplification and summarization is to reduce syntactic or structural complexities while preserving the central meaning or relevant information in the given text. Unfortunately, syntactic simplification algorithms often assume a uniform treatment of syntactic structures. This is especially true in the domain of relative clauses.

Relative clauses are often considered to contain parenthetical information. That is, their putative role in the sentence is to provide background information about the mentioned entity or entities. Consider (1): [1]

(1) You [get] a guy down the street **who comes up, uh, carrying a knife**.[2]

[1] Relative clauses are shown in boldface and the referent noun phrase is underlined. The matrix verb, the verb of the sentence in which the relative clause is embedded, is in brackets.

[2] Unless otherwise noted, all examples in this paper are taken from the Switchboard Treebank corpus (Godfrey et al. 1992, Marcus et al. 1993), a syntactically parsed version of the Switchboard corpus of American English telephone conversations.

Proceedings of the NAACL HLT Workshop on Extracting and Using Constructions in Computational Linguistics, pages 17–24,
Los Angeles, California, June 2010.

According to the above definition of relative clauses, they key information in (1) is in the main clause *You get a guy down the street*. That is, (1) means something like: the entity *you* comes to possess *a guy down the street*. If we accordingly consider the relative clause as the background or incidental information and remove it from the semantic analysis, the assertion – the key piece of the information – would be lost.

In this paper, we discuss the Presentational Relative Clause (PRC) construction, as seen in (1). In the PRC, the relative clause, rather than the main clause, contains the assertion of the utterance (Duffield & Michaelis, 2009). Moreover, we analyze the construction in detail to assess its potential usefulness in NLP applications. Based on linguistic analysis, we suggest features that may be useful for implementation of automatic identification of PRC constructions. We believe that the identification of this construction will be useful in discriminating central information units from the peripheral ones.

2 Relative Clauses

Relative clauses are constructions in which a verbal clause modifies a nominal element, the "head," as shown in (2) and (3):

(2) I [like] cars **that _____ are designed with human beings in mind**.
(3) I [like] those movies **that you watch ____ time and time again**.

In (2), the relative clause *that are designed with human beings in mind* describes the head nominal *cars*, while in (3), the head nominal *those movies* is described by the relative clause *that you watch time and time again.* The gap in the relative clause indicating the position of the co-referential noun phrase is shown.

Relative clauses are typically embedded in main clauses, with the result that the nominal element satisfies a semantic-role requirement of two different verbs. For example, consider sentence (2), where the head nominal *cars* serves as an argument of the verb *like* while a gap that shares its referent with the head nominal marks the argument of the passive verb *designed.* Likewise, in (3) the referent shared by the head nominal *those movies* in the main clause and the gap in the relative clause satisfies the requirements of two separate verbs, *like* and *watch.*

2.1 Types of Relative Clauses

In the linguistic tradition, relative clauses are typically classified into restrictive and non-restrictive types, as seen in (4-5), respectively.

(4) And, you know, I [want] a car **that I can work on** _____, because I think it just costs too much even to get the oil changed anymore.
(5) And once you've [reached] the river walk area, **which ____ is the tourist area**, it's usually pretty safe during the day.

In (4), the speaker has asserted that he would like a car; the restrictive relative clause specifies the type of car as one belonging to the set of cars that he could work on, as opposed to a type of car that he would be unable to repair. In (5), the relative clause does not identify the river walk area as one out of a set of areas, but simply provides additional information about it. In neither case does the relative clause assert information in the discourse; rather, it expresses a presupposed proposition (e.g., 'I can work on x,''x is the tourist area') that is assumed to be known by both the speaker and the addressee.

Accordingly, relative clauses are assumed to provide background information concerning the entities they modify. This background material serves either to distinguish the referent from others of its kind, as in a restrictive relative clause, or provide additional material, as in a non-restrictive relative clause, rather than asserting something new about the referent.

2.2 Relative Clauses in NLP

In line with the linguistic consensus, work in NLP has also viewed relative clauses as expressing background information about a referent. In syntactic simplification, the structural complexity is resolved by splitting a sentence into multiple ones (Siddharthan, 2003; Chandrasekar, 1996). In effect, the relative clause is pulled out of the main clause into an independent sentence. For example, (5) would be simplified into (6).

(6) And once you've reached the river walk area, it's usually pretty safe during the day. **The river walk area is the tourist area**.

In text summarization, where background information is considered parenthetical and identified with non-key content, relative clauses are simply disregarded (Siddharthan et al., 2004). That is, if we consider the relative clause to contain parenthetical information, it is reasonable to simply remove the non-key content from the text prior to any semantic analysis.

3 Presentational Relative Clauses

As the analysis of (1) above suggests, however, not all relative clauses contain parenthetical information. In fact, many linguistic studies have argued that subordinate clauses can make assertions (Goldberg, 2006; Menn, 1974; McCawley, 1981; Fox & Thompson, 1990), as a counterpoint to the studies that view them as expressing exclusively backgrounded information (Shibatani, 2009).

Here, in line with Michaelis and Lambrecht (1996), Kay and Fillmore (1999) and other work in the Construction Grammar tradition, we analyze a particular construction, the Presentational Relative Clause construction (PRC), as a productive idiomatic pattern. The PRC is a construction in which the material presented in the relative clause is not backgrounded, either in the sense of being unnecessary parenthetical material, or in the sense of being already known to both speaker and addressee (Duffield & Michaelis, 2009). In the PRC, information is asserted in the relative clause that modifies the nominal element, which is introduced by a semantically bleached main clause. Examples of the PRC include (1) and the following:

(7) They [had] some guy **that ___ was defending himself**.
(8) And I [know] people **who ___have been drug tested and who have not, you know, been hired by a corporation**.
(9) And they've [got] a fifteen year old **that ___'s their boss that ___ is carrying a gun**

Each of the examples above were examined in their original contexts to determining that an uninformative main clause introduces the head nominal, while an assertion is contained within the relative clause. In (7), the main clause that introduces the referent *some guy* is semantically uninformative. By this we mean that it does NOT assert that the entity *they* possessed *some guy*. Rather, the asserted proposition in the utterance is in the relative clause, and (7) can be paraphrased as *A guy was defending himself.* In (8) the important information is not that the speaker knows a certain set of people. Instead, the key assertion here is: "Some people have been drug tested and have not been hired by a corporation." Likewise, (9), illustrating what might be described as a double-PRC, could be rephrased as, "A fifteen-year-old is their boss and is carrying a gun."

3.1 Anatomy of the PRC construction

The PRC construction is typically characterized by three main properties: a semantically empty main clause, a head nominal in the object position of the main clause that is newly introduced into the discourse, and a subject-gap relative clause that modifies the head nominal.

First property: The semantically bleached main clause serves to convey the restriction on the range of the existential quantifier rather than an assertion. In (7), for example, the main clause conveys the restriction 'x is a guy'. Consequently, a PRC, unlike a restrictive relative, is not optional. It is a required part of the clause in which it appears, exemplified by the fact that (7) cannot reasonably be construed as asserting 'They had some guy'.

Being uninformative, the main verbs of PRC tend to have low semantic weight, as in (10-12).

(10) I've [seen] some statistics **that ___ say it's more expensive to kill somebody than to keep them in prison for life**.
(11) You [get] a guy down the street **who ___ comes up, uh, carrying a knife.**
(12) When our kids were small we [had] a couple of, uh, good women **who ___ would often come to the house**.

The bracketed main verbs in (10-12), which otherwise denote relations of perception, obtaining, and possession, respectively, here appear simply to 'set the stage' for their object referents. In other words, (10) does not assert that the speaker sees something, (11) does not assert that the addressee obtains something and (12) does not assert that some people possessed someone. Rather than predicating a property or action of the main clause subject, the main clause predications in (10-12) provide an explicit or inferred center of perspective from which to view the entity denoted by the head nominal (Koenig and Lambrecht, 1999).

Second property: The discourse-new head nominal is in the object position of the main clause. Thus, the PRC enables the speaker to avoid violating a hearer-based information-packaging constraint that Lambrecht (1994) refers to as the Principle of Separation of Reference and Role (PSRR): "Do not introduce a referent and talk about it in the same clause" (ibid). In other words, to aid the hearer in anchoring the new referent in discourse, the speaker introduces it in the object position of the main clause, and then predicates upon it in the relative clause, as in example (13):

(13) *Speaker A:* We have more options now then (sic) we did when my kids were born, with being able to take off full-time longer, you can phase your schedule in so that it 's not full-time for up to six months.
Speaker B: Oh boy, that's great.
Speaker A: It 's really neat. I've [had] a couple of assistants **that ___ came back just three days a week** or they've, you know, whatever schedule they want from a pay standpoint.

Consider Speaker A's second turn, restructured as a declarative clause rather than as a PRC, and thus violating the PSRR. This time the assertion is conveyed in the main clause, but with the new entity in the in the subject position the result is pragmatically awkward:

(14) *Speaker A:* It 's really neat. ***A couple of assistants came back just three days a week*** or they've, you know, whatever schedule they want from a pay standpoint.

An additional example is provided in (15):

(15) *Speaker B*: I've never liked D.C. a whole lot and a really hate the Redskins. And a lot of it's because, you know, I [got] a lot of people, you know, at work with and everything **that __ are big Redskin fans**. (*??A lot of people I work with and everything are big Redskin fans.*)

Thus, a crucial identifying characteristic of the PRC is that it always modifies head nominals that are main-clause objects.

Third property: Third identifying property of the PRC is the presence of a subject-gap relative clause. That is, the relative clause modifying the head nominal contains a gap in the subject position of the relative clause that is co-referential with the head nominal, as in (7) repeated here as (16):

(16) They [had] some guy **that ___ was defending himself**.

There are, however, cases in which the head nominal is modified by an object-gap relative clause, which conveys an assertion, as in (17):

(17) Everybody [gets] five pounds of garbage **that they can throw away____** you know uh but more than that every week uh you've got to pay by the pound.

In the example above, as with the more prototypical subject-gap PRC, the main clause does not make an assertion (in this case, the main clause does not assert that everybody receives five pounds of garbage). Rather, the assertion in the relative clause is demonstrated by the appropriate paraphrase, "Everybody can throw away five pounds of garbage." While speakers do produce object-gap sentences to convey assertions, subject-gap PRC tokens account for the majority of assertoric relative clauses in spoken discourse (Duffield and Michaelis, 2009). This results in the subject-gap structure being a useful property for identifying prototypical instances of the PRC.

4 Why identify the PRC construction?

As argued above, identifying the PRC is important because, unlike restrictive and non-restrictive relative clauses, the PRC does not present backgrounded or parenthetical information. Rather, the loss of information asserted in a PRC results in the loss of inferences crucial for the discourse.

4.1 "My son is an animal lover."

So far we have seen sentences or utterances that would inarguably be interpreted as sentences containing a PRC. However, there are PRCs, which, while equipped with every relevant PRC characteristic, initially appear to contain relative clauses expressing parenthetical information. Consider the following sentence:

(18) I [had] a son, he's now gone from the home, **that ___ was an animal lover**.

In isolation, (18) could be interpreted as asserting that the speaker has a son, who now happens to have left home. The relative clause *that was an animal lover* would be treated as background information about the son. Yet an examination of the context of the conversation reveals that the relative clause contains crucial information with regard to the discourse as a whole:

(19) *Speaker A*: Do you want to hear about my other animals I've had?
Speaker B: Sure, sure.
Speaker A: I've had a skunk
Speaker B: Yeah.
Speaker A: I've had a Burmese python, I've had rats, I've had mice.
Speaker B: Wow.
Speaker A: Uh, let's see, I've had gerbils, I have, I [had] a son, he's now gone from the home, **that ___ was an animal lover**.
Speaker B: Uh-huh.
Speaker A: So at one point I had a snake, skunk, dog and a cat running loose in the house.

In this case, we see even a more compelling reason to identify this sentence as a PRC. Disregarding the relative clause in (18) and treating the main clause as containing an asserted proposition, results in a radically different reading: the speaker's son is among the animals that the speaker claims to have owned (i.e. "I've had a skunk, I've had a Burmese python, I've had rats, I've had mice, I've had gerbils, I had a son…"). By classifying this sentence as a PRC, we reach the intended assertion, "My son was an animal lover," which in turn explains why the speaker has been the proud owner of a menagerie of animals.

4.2 Other examples

Much like the example in (18), the discourse context of the other PRCs presented in this paper substantiates the claim that they present information central to the discourse. The PRC in (7) "They [had] some guy **that was defending himself,**" used in a conversation describing a trial, signals that the situation departs from the prototypical courtroom schema in a crucial respect (the defendant is without a lawyer).

Other instances of the PRC, such as (8) "And I [know] people **who ___have been drug tested and who have not, you know, been hired by a corporation**," like (18), provide explanatory information: the reason for the speaker's negative view of drug-testing. Finally, in (15) "I [got] a lot of people, you know, at work with and everything **that ___ are big Redskin fans**," the PRC utterance explains why the speaker dislikes a particular football team. Treating these clauses as background information, restricting categories of entities, or removing them from semantic analysis results in the loss of information about causal connections in the text.

5 Identifying the PRC construction

Thus far we have presented the identifying linguistic properties of the PRC constructions. We will now demonstrate how these properties (see Section 3.1) lend themselves to features that could be useful for automatic identification and classification of PRCs. For the purposes of this section we make the assumption that we will only retain instances that can be parsed by an automatic parser (Collins 1999, Charniak, 1997). The features we suggest are based on the results of a corpus study carried out by Duffield and Michaelis (in prep) examining the role of the PRC in the distribution of relative clause types in spoken discourse.

5.1 The distribution of the PRC in discourse

In the study by Duffield and Michaelis (2009, in prep), 1000 sentences (500 each of subject-gap and object-gap relative clauses) from the Switchboard Corpus (Godfrey, 1996) were manually examined for the first two of the identifying properties of PRC tokens as described in Section 3.1. In addition, each of the 1000 sentences was examined within a context of 50 lines of previous discourse to determine whether or not the relative clause conveyed an assertion.

Their results showed that three properties, namely, a semantically bleached verb, discourse-new head nominals, and an assertion in the relative clause, were found to significantly predict relative clauses of the subject-gap type, suggesting that PRCs account for the prevalence of subject-gap relative clauses in discourse. In fact, 22.4% of subject-gap relative clauses were PRCs, while only 6.8% of object-gap relative clauses displayed features of the PRC. The manner in which Duffield and Michaelis manually annotated their data, although based on linguistic analysis as discussed above, easily lends itself to a list of properties that could be automatically used to identify PRCs in larger corpora.

5.2 Verb in the main clause

Corresponding to the first property (Section 3.1) of a semantically empty main clause, Duffield & Michaelis have observed that PRC tokens have the tendency to co-occur with verbs of existence, perception and discovery. Table 1 lists these verbs.

Be	Get	See	Hear	Tell
Have	Find	Know	Look	Wonder

Table 1: Main-clause verbs likely to appear in PRCs.

This suggests that encoding the lemmatized verbs as features may help in automatic classification of PRCs.

5.3 Position of head nominal

The head nominal of the relative clause was found to occur in two positions relative to the main-clause verb. It was either the second argument of the main-clause verb (20) or the complement in the prepositional phrase (21), which in turn was the second argument of the main-clause verb.

(20) They [had] {some guy **that ___ was defending himself**.}-NP

(21) I have a friend who was [telling] me {about her brother **who ___ gets high all the time**.}-PP

Duffield and Michaelis also observed that there was a correlation between the main-clause verb and the position in which the head nominal was found. That is, the verbs such as *look, tell,* and *wonder* were regularly found when the head nominal was the complement in the PP, while other verbs in Table 1 more frequently occurred with the head nominal in the direct argument position of the main-clause verb.

Furthermore, Duffield and Michaelis found that in cases where the head nominal was the complement of the PP, the head of the PP was found to be either *of* or *about.*

This suggests that in conjunction with the features derived from the lemmatized verb, the position of the head nominal in relation to the main-clause verb could be encoded as a feature. That is, for each of the sentences examined, a feature can be coded for either a NP complement or PP complement, given which type of complement the relative clause sits in.

In addition to the position of the head nominal, for those relative clauses that are found in the PP complement a feature can also be coded for the preposition heading the phrase.

5.4 Head nominal: noun and modifiers

Corresponding to the second property (Section 3.1) of PRCs, discourse-new status of modified head nominals, is indefinite form. Although Duffield & Michaelis recognize that the distinction between the 'given' and 'new' discourse statuses is not the same thing as definite versus indefinite form, discourse-active entities tend to be formally marked as definite, while discourse-new entities tend to be marked as indefinite (Prince 1992).

Head nominals considered as indefinite include bare plural nouns (e.g., *engineers*), determinerless nominals modified by adjectives or cardinal numbers (e.g., *about forty kindergarteners*), bare mass nouns (e.g., *material*), nominals with weak quantifiers (e.g., *some companies*), indefinite pronouns (e.g., *somebody, anybody*) and nominals containing the indefinite article *a* (e.g., *a fish*).

Definite head nominals include those containing the definite article *the* (e.g., *the thing, the resources*), demonstrative determiners (e.g., *this recording, that attitude*), possessive determiners (e.g., *my bass*), strong quantifiers (e.g., *every story, all these people*), demonstrative pronouns (e.g., *that, those*) and proper nouns (e.g., *Rockport, Albany*). Partitive nominal expressions with indefinite heads (e.g., *one of those things*, *some of my friends*) are also considered as indefinite.

To turn the above into linguistic features that are characteristic of definite and indefinite head nominals, we suggest a number of possible features for classification. Several of these relating to the head noun phrase may contribute to the identification of PRCs:

Head nominal features:

- the phrasal categories of the sisters to the noun in the head noun phrase. These features will encode the presence of any adjectival or prepositional phrases within the head noun phrase. The inclusion of these features will account for the existence of any adjectival modification on the head noun phrase and/or partitive nominals.
- the existence of named entities in the head noun phrase to ascertain the existence of any proper nouns in the head nominal.

Head nominal features encoding:

- whether or not the nominal is a pronoun. This will serve to introduce the indefinite and demonstrative pronouns into the classification of PRCs.
- singularity/plurarity of the head nominal.

Modifier features encoding:

- articles and determiners,
- quantifiers, and
- possessive pronouns that modify the head noun or noun phrase.

5.5 Gap in the relative clause

The third and final property shared by PRCs concerns the gap in the relative clause. The gap occurs in subject position and is co-referential with the head nominal. This can be identified in the syntactic parses by the presence of a trace in the syntactic position co-indexed[3] with the relative pronouns *that, who,* or *which.*

The syntactic position of the gap can be coded as a feature. These would also include a feature for cases where the gap is entirely missing from the relative clause. This is to account for cases of relative clauses containing a pronoun in the position where the gap should be (e.g. The gap in this example is filled with the pronoun *it*: "Here['s] a journal **that I'm in the board of *it*.**").

5.6 Subject position of matrix clause

In addition to the above features, based on Duffield & Michaelis' characterization of the PRC, there is one other syntactic characteristic worth investigating—the subject of the matrix clause. Consider the following PRCs:

(22) *They* [had] some guy **that ___ was defending himself.**

(23) *There*['s] a lot of people **that fall into that category**

(24) *It* [was] a moving man ____ **pulled right up to her house, broke in and stole everything she owned[4].**

General observation of PRCs is that they seem to display a tendency to have either a pronoun (22), or an expletive *there* (23) or *it* (24) in the subject position of the matrix clause. This suggests that the lexical content of the subject position may be a useful predictor for PRC classification.

6 Discussion and Conclusion

In this paper, we have presented identifying properties of the PRC construction. We recognize that individual properties as presented here contribute to but do not determine the final meaning of the PRC construction as a whole, but in combination, they are likely predictors. Not all syntactic forms can be treated in the same way. By not privileging the syntactic level, but rather treating lexical, morphological, and syntactic features equally, we are able to identify key indicators that could be used to identify the function of a relative clause in discourse as conveying an assertion as opposed to backgrounded information.

3 Note that coindexation is distinct from coreference. In Treebank, coindexation involves the creation of a syntactic link between the trace and the constituent that was moved out of the position trace now occupies. Coreference is the relationship between the gap and the referent. Most parsers, however, do not supply co-indexation.

4 Certain types of PRCs, such as in this example, are produced without the relative pronoun. Such PRCs are referred to as amalgams (see Lambrecht, 1988 for discussion)

For the purposes of NLP, we must work within the framework of phrasal structures, constrained by the resources currently available. Yet as we have suggested here, those resources, although not constructionally based, can be used to identify constructions for the purpose of extracting relevant information from naturally occurring data. We have further investigated the applicability of a construction-based approach to identifying relative clause types when the individual components, such as lexical items themselves are not themselves effective predictors. This clause-level information allows for richer representations of textual meaning.

Our future plans include experiments with implementing automatic classifiers of relative clause type based on these features. Such empirical study will give us a better understanding of the degree of usefulness of these features in identifying PRCs in text data. We anticipate that additional features will be discovered during the implementation process.

Acknowledgements

We would like to thank Martha Palmer, Jim Martin, Jinho Choi, Susan Brown, Les Sikos, and Steve Duman for valuable feedback.

References

Chandrasekar, Raman, and Bangalore Srinivas. 1997. Automatic Induction of Rules for Text Simplification. *Knowledge-Based Systems*, 10(3): 183-190.

Chandrasekar, Raman, Christine Doran, and Bangalore Srinivas. 1996. Motivations and Methods for Text Simplification. In *Proceedings of the 16th International Conference on Computational Linguistics (COLING 1996)*, pages 1041-1044, Copenhagen, Denmark.

Charniak, Eugene. 2000. A Maximum-Entropy-Inspired Parser. In *Proceedings of NAACL00*, pages 132-139, Seattle, WA, USA.

Collins, Michael John. 1999. Head-Driven Statistical Models for Natural Language Parsing. Ph.D. thesis, University of Pennsylvania, Philadelphia, PA.

Devlin, Siobhan, and Gary Unthank. 2006. Helping Aphasic People Process Online Information. In *Proceedings of the Eighth International ACM SIGACCESS Conference on Computers and Accessibility*, pages 225-226, Portland, OR, USA.

Duffield, Cecily Jill and Laura A. Michaelis. 2009. Why Subject Relatives Prevail: Constraints versus Constructional Licensing. Presented at the *2009 Annual Meeting of the Linguistics Society of America. San Francisco*. CA, USA

Duffield, Cecily Jill and Laura A. Michaelis. in prep. Why Subject Relatives Prevail: Constraints versus Constructional Licensing.

Kay, Paul and Charles J. Fillmore. 1999. Grammatical Constructions and Linguistic Generalizations: the What's X doing Y? Construction. *Language,* 75(1):1-33.

Fox, Barbara, and Sandra Thompson. 1990. A Discourse Explanation of the Grammar of Relative Clauses in English Conversation. *Language* 66:51-64

Goldberg, Adele E. 2006. *Constructions at work. The nature of generalization in language*. Oxford University Press, Oxford.

Menn, Lise. 1974. Assertions not made by the main clause of a sentence. *Studies in the Linguistic Sciences (University of Illinois)* 4(1):132-143.

Koenig, Jean-Pierre and Knud Lambrecht. 1999. French Relative Clauses as Secondary Predicates. In Francis Corbin, Carmen Dobrovie-Sorin, and Jean-Marie Marandin, editors, *Empirical issues in Formal Syntax and Semantics 2*. Thesus, pages 191-214, The Hague, The Netherlands.

Lambrecht, Knud. 1994. Information structure and sentence form: Topic, focus, and the mental representation of discourse referents. In *Cambridge Studies in Linguistics* 71. Cambridge, Cambridge University Press.

Lambrecht, Knud. 1988. There was a Farmer had a Dog: Syntactic Amalgams Revisited. In S. Axmaker, A. Jaisser and H. Singmaster, editors, *The Proceedings of the Fourteenth Annual Meeting of the Berkeley Linguistics Society*. BLS, Inc., pages 319-339 Berkeley, CA.

McCawley, James D. 1981. The Syntax and Semantics of English Relative Clauses. *Lingua,* 53: 99-149.

Michaelis, Laura A. and Knud Lambrecht. 1996. The Exclamative Sentence Type in English. In Adele Goldberg, editor, *Conceptual Structure, Discourse and Language*. Center for the Study of Language and Information, pages 375-389, Stanford, CA.

Petersen, Sarah E. and Mari Ostendorf. 2007. Text simplification for language learners: a corpus analysis. In *SLaTE-2007*, pages 69-72, Farmington, PA.

Siddharthan, Advaith. 2003. Syntactic simplification and Text Cohesion. Ph.D. thesis, University of Cambridge, UK.

Siddharthan, Advaith, Ani Nenkova and Kathleen McKeown. 2004. Syntactic Simplification for Improving Content Selection in Multi-Document Summarization. In *Proceedings of the 20th International Conference on Computational Linguistics (COLING 2004*), Geneva, Switzerland.

StringNet as a Computational Resource for Discovering and Investigating Linguistic Constructions

David Wible **Nai-Lung Tsao**
National Central University
No.300, Jhongda Rd.
Jhongli City, Taoyuan County 32001, Taiwan
wible@stringnet.org beaktsao@stringnet.org

Abstract

We describe and motivate the design of a lexico-grammatical knowledgebase called StringNet and illustrate its significance for research into constructional phenomena in English. StringNet consists of a massive archive of what we call hybrid n-grams. Unlike traditional n-grams, hybrid n-grams can consist of any co-occurring combination of POS tags, lexemes, and specific word forms. Further, we detect and represent superordinate and subordinate relations among hybrid n-grams by cross-indexing, allowing the navigation of StringNet through these hierarchies, from specific fixed expressions ("It's the thought that counts") up to their hosting proto-constructions (e.g. the It Cleft construction: "it's the [noun] that [verb]"). StringNet supports discovery of grammatical dependencies (e.g., subject-verb agreement) in non-canonical configurations as well as lexical dependencies (e.g., adjective/noun collocations specific to families of constructions).

1 Introduction

Constructions have posed persistent challenges to the field of computational linguistics (Baldwin et al 2004; Sag et al 2002; Zhang et al 2006). Challenges to both statistical and symbolic approaches arise, for example, from the meager degree of productivity and non-canonical structures of many constructions and, as a loosely defined family of linguistic phenomena, their varied mix of regularity and idiomicity (Fillmore, Kay, and O'Connor 1988). It has been argued for decades that constructions are central rather than peripheral to any adequate account of linguistic knowledge and that they pose substantial challenges to mainstream accounts of language (Bolinger, 1977, 1985; Fillmore, Kay, and O'Connor, 1988; Goldberg, 1995; inter alia). But the recent attention they have been receiving in computational research is perhaps due more to their status as troublemakers (or a "pain in the neck", Sag et al 2002). Baldwin et al (2004) found, for example, that 39% of parse failures on clean data (BNC) occurred on constructions. (See Zhang et al (2006) for other such findings.) Thus, it is becoming urgent to "deal with" constructions for the sake of NLP. In this paper, however, we would like to shift perspective a bit to explore instead the application of computational resources for the sake of constructions. Our longer term aim is to broaden and deepen research on constructions in order to support the learning and teaching of constructions in second language education. Two basic challenges we address are: (1) the varied mix of regularity and idiomicity to be found within the wide range of constructions in a language (Fillmore, Kay, and O'Connor, 1988; Jackendoff, 2008 inter alia), and (2) the inheritance-like hierarchical relations holding between and among different constructions as instances of more general constructions or proto-constructions subsuming other constructions as sub-cases (Goldberg 1995 inter alia). To address these, we introduce a lexico-grammatical knowledgebase called StringNet and describe some ways that it can support the investigation of constructions.

Within the broad range of definitions for constructions, one widely shared premise is that the traditional division between lexical knowledge on the one hand and grammatical rules on the other is an artificial one. There are huge tracts of linguistic territory lying between the lexical and the grammatical which usage-attuned linguists have seen as not simply a residue of undiscovered deeper general principles but as the actual lay of the linguistic land (Bolinger 1977). We have taken this lexico-grammatical territory as a core target of the work we report here. StringNet has been designed to

Proceedings of the NAACL HLT Workshop on Extracting and Using Constructions in Computational Linguistics, pages 25–31,
Los Angeles, California, June 2010.

provide traction on some of this intermediate terrain.

The paper is organized as follows. Section 2 describes and motivates the basic approach we have taken in designing StringNet. Section 3 describes the design of StringNet itself. In Section 4, we illustrate the significance of StringNet for construction research with some extended examples. Section 5 is the conclusion.

2 Background and Approach

The specific approach we take to designing StringNet is motivated by the varied mixture of idiomicity and regularity exhibited by constructions mentioned above and the problems this poses both for symbolic and statistical approaches in computational linguistics. To frame the properties of constructions that we hope StringNet can help address, we make use of Fillmore, Kay, and O'Connor's distinction between substantive and formal idioms (1988), the latter of which they categorize eventually under "grammatical constructions" (p. 506). Substantive (or "lexically filled") idioms are those fixed at the lexical level, that is, lexical strings relatively frozen except perhaps for inflectional variation. Among examples they site are *pull a fast one*, *all of a sudden*, *kick the bucket*. Others, extracted by StringNet, would include *as a matter of fact*, *at a moment's notice*, *just to be on the safe side*, and a massive inventory of other fixed strings. In contrast to substantive idioms, formal (or "lexically open") idioms "…are syntactic patterns dedicated to semantic and pragmatic purposes not knowable from their form alone" (p. 505) These would include such expressions detected with StringNet as "bring [pnp[1]] to [dps] senses," "stop [pnp] in [dps] tracks," "It is safe to [verb] that" (e.g., *It is safe to assume/say/predict that*)," "There is a tendency for [noun] to [verb]," "[verb][dps] socks off" (e.g., *knock your socks off*). As mentioned above, on Fillmore et al's analysis, it is the latter type, the formal idioms, which are eventually "absorbed into the category of grammatical constructions" (p. 506). Crucially for us, however, they point out the potential significance of substantive (lexically filled) idioms for construction research. A substantive or frozen idiom may be a sub-case of a formal or lexically open idiom. Our example of this is the lexically filled idiom "It's the thought that counts" with its idiosyncratic interpretation that must be learned as a listeme; it presupposes something substandard about a gift or an effort as well as forgiveness of this in light of the good intentions of the giver. Yet much of its meaning derives from its status as an instance of the more general "It cleft" construction; the focus slot hosts one member of a contrasting pair or set, and that member is assumed to be new information, etc.).

Considering the challenges of extracting and representing these two sorts of expressions, substantive idioms have been the far more tractable of the two. Specifically, substantive, lexically filled idioms are readily susceptible to detection and representation by traditional n-grams. It is formal (lexically open) idioms, however, which have been identified more closely with constructions, yet they have proven much more resistant to extraction by computational means; for example, approaches using n-grams have so far shown little progress in handling this category of expression. And parsers famously have difficulties with their non-canonical structures (Baldwin et al 2004; Zhang et al 2006; inter alia).

The design of StringNet is aimed at addressing three long-recognized qualities of constructions: (1) the non-canonical structures of many of them; (2) their syntagmatic mixing of fixed and substitutable slots, making them resistant to representation by traditional n-grams; and (3) the hierarchical relations holding among them, as, for example, "it's the thought that counts" instantiates the general It Cleft construction while each arguably warrants independent status as a construction.

3 Design and Construction of StringNet

3.1 Overview

In this section we describe the design of StringNet. In light of the well-documented problems that constructions pose for parsers, we eschew parsing at this stage to see what we can achieve without it first.[2] StringNet is a corpus-derived knowledge-

[1] The glosses for the POS tags appearing in the paper, taken from CLAWS 5 tagset is are follows: pnp = pronoun, dps = possessive determiner, nn1 = singular noun, nn2 = plural noun, vvz = present 3rd person singular verb; vm0 = modal verb.

[2] StringNet will provide some natural spaces where shallow parsing could play a well-motivated role, but we leave that for future work.

base, automatically extracted from the British National Corpus (BNC). The structure of StringNet can be described in two parts: (1) a special type of n-grams that we refer to as hybrid n-grams, constituting the core content of StringNet and (2) the inter-relations among these hybrid n-grams, represented by cross-indexing. We describe and motivate these two aspects in turn.

3.2 Hybrid n-grams

Unlike traditional n-grams, hybrid n-grams can consist of co-occurring grams from different levels of analysis, more specifically, a combination of lexemes, word forms, and parts of speech (POSs) potentially side by side within the same string. For example, "from my point of view" is a traditional n-gram attested in BNC, where the grams are all lexical. However, our hybrid n-gram extraction, in addition, detects the substitutability of the second slot in this string and indicates this substitutability by a POS in that position: "from [dps] point of view". By including POS categories, hybrid n-grams can encode the paradigmatic dimension in addition to the syntagmatic one represented by traditional n-grams.

The hybrid n-grams that constitute StringNet's content are derived from BNC. Specifically, we include any contiguous combination of gram types ranging from bi-grams to 8-grams. Two criteria must be met for each hybrid n-gram. (1) It must include at least one lexical gram in the string (that is, either a lexeme or a specific word form). This means that all of the hybrid n-grams are "lexically anchored" to some extent. And (2) it must be attested in BNC at a minimum frequency of five tokens.

There are four categories of grams that can occur in the hybrid n-grams of StringNet. From specific to general, these categories are: (1) word form (thus, *ran*, *run*, and *running* are three distinct word forms); (2) lexeme (**run**, including all its different inflectional forms: *run*, *ran*, *running*); these are indicated in bold to distinguish them from word forms; (3) detailed POS category, taken from the large CLAWS set of 46 tags ([nn1] for singular noun); these are marked off in brackets; (4) rough POS category, taken from abbreviated tagset of 12 POS tags ([noun], including plural and singular nouns); indicated with brackets as well to avoid flooding users with too many distinctions in the representations. Further, each hybrid n-gram is indexed to all tokens instantiating it in BNC. Thus, every token of "saw the light" occurring in BNC is indexed to all hybrid n-grams that it satisfies, for example, indexed to "[verb] the light", "**see** [det] light", "[verb] [det] light", "saw the [noun]", and so on. As mentioned above, only hybrid n-grams attested by at least five tokens occurring in BNC are kept in StringNet.

3.3 Structure of StringNet: Cross-indexing of Hybrid n-grams

Since the inventory of gram types consists of four categories and these can stand in subordinate and superordinate relation to each other, it becomes possible to find relations of inclusion or subsumption between hybrid n-grams. For the sake of simplicity in the user interface, we label these as parent/child relations.

Take the tri-gram "paying attention to" as an example. As a string of word forms, this hybrid n-gram can be considered a child of the hybrid n-grams: **pay** attention to (where **pay** indicates the lexeme and includes forms pay, paid, paying). Non-monotonically, then, "paying attention to" can (and does) have more than one parent, for example: **pay** [noun] to; **pay** attention [prep]; among several others. StringNet exhaustively cross-indexes all of these thus-related hybrid n-grams. (Note that hybrid n-grams can have more complicated relations with each other, but these are not indexed in the current StringNet.) As a massive inventory of hybrid n-grams and the cross-indexing among them, StringNet is very large. For comparison, the size of our POS-tagged BNC is 4.4 GB. StringNet, which we extracted from BNC, is over a terabyte (over 1,000 GB), about 250 times the size of BNC.

The hybrid n-grams making up StringNet were extracted from BNC on the simple criterion of frequency (minimum frequency of 5 tokens in BNC), making no use of statistical techniques such as word association measures in the extraction process. However, to support queries of StringNet we must have some criteria for ranking the hybrid n-grams returned in a query result. For this, we use MI as our default hybrid n-gram association measurement. The MI equation is as follows:

$$MI = \log\left(\frac{P(X)}{P(x_1)P(x_2)...P(x_n)}\right)$$

,where $X = x_1x_2...x_n$

This equation is well-known as an association measure for collocations consisting of word pairs. However it is not appropriate directly used in measuring hybrid n-grams or n-grams in Lex-Checker because it cannot compare n-grams of different length, i.e with different values of n. It would typically be biased toward longer n-grams. Therefore we use a version which normalizes, as follows:

$$Normalized\, MI(h_n, q) = \frac{MI(h_n)}{\max MI_n(q)}$$

,where h_n is the target hybrid n-gram, q is user query, *MI*( ) is the traditional MI equation mentioned above and maxMI_n is the maximum MI score achieved among all of the n-grams of any given length n and retrieved for query q.

For example, a hybrid tri-gram T="pay attention to" and a hybrid 4-gram Q="pay attention to the" will be shown in the results of the query q="attention". Assume $MI(T)$=5, $MI(Q)$=7, max-MI_3 ("attention") =15 and maxMI_4 ("attention") = 20. Then the *Normalized* $MI(T,q)$ = 5/15 = 0.334 and *Normalized* $MI(Q,q)$ = 7/20 = 0.35. So we can rank Q higher than T. $MI(h_n)$ will never be greater than max$MI_n(q)$ because by stipulation, max$MI_n(q)$ represents the highest MI score of all n-grams at a given value of n and a query q. So Normalized MI will always fall between 0 and 1. This creates a common specified range within which MI scores for hybrid n-grams of different lengths can be ranked. It is important to note that this ranking measure is not incorporated into StringNet itself (e.g., as a criterion for hybrid n-grams to be included in StringNet). Rather it is a post hoc means of ranking search results. StringNet is compatible with other methods of ranking and contains all statistical information needed to run such alternative measures.

3.4 Pruning

As we mention above, hybrid n-grams in StringNet consist of all possible combinations of word form, lexeme and two types of POS in strings from 2 to 8 grams in length. Thus for every single traditional n-gram consisting of a string of word forms, there are numerous hybrid n-grams that also describe that same string. For a traditional 8-gram, for example, we create $4^7 \times 2$=32768 different hybrid n-grams (taking into account our criterion that at least one token has to be a word form or lexeme). Such a large amount of information will cause low performance of the StringNet applications. In order to decrease the search space while still keeping most of the useful information, we introduce pruning. Specifically, pruning is intended to eliminate redundant hybrid n-grams from searches or applications of StringNet. There are two types of pruning we use in StringNet currently: Vertical pruning and Horizontal pruning.

Vertical pruning:
Vertical pruning considers pairs of hybrid n-grams that are identical in length and differ in the identity of some gram in the sequence. Consider the following such pair.

a. hybrid n-gram 1: my point [prep] view
b. hybrid n-gram 2: my point of view

These 4-grams are identical except for the third gram; moreover, the counterpart grams occupying that third slot ("of" and [prep]) stand in an inclusion relation, "of" being a member of the POS category [prep]. Recalling our cross-indexing, this parenthood relation between such hybrid n-grams can be readily detected. Pruning of the parent occurs in cases where a threshold proportion of the instances attested in BNC of that parent are also instances of the child. Consider (a) and (b) above. Here the parent (a) "my point [prep] view" would be pruned since all cases of [prep] in this pattern in BNC are indeed cases of the preposition "of". Consider now (c), another parent hybrid n-gram of (b) that, in contrast, would not be pruned.

c. hybrid n-gram 3: [dps] point of view

This parent is retained because "my" accounts for fewer than 80% of the instances of the [dps] in this pattern. The retention of "[dps] point of view" indicates that more than one possessive pronoun is attested in the [dps] slot of this string in a threshold proportion of its cases and thus the slot shows substitutability. In a word, vertical pruning eliminates hybrid n-grams containing POS grams which do not represent attested substitutability. Currently, for our StringNet search interface (LexChecker) we prune parents with children that represent over 80% of the BNC tokens also described by that parent.

Horizontal pruning:

The main idea of Horizontal pruning is the same as Vertical pruning. The only difference is the axis of comparison: For horizontal pruning, two hybrid n-grams for comparison differ only by value of n (ie., by length). For example, comparing the hybrid n-gram "[dps] point of" and "[dps] point of view," the shorter one is parent and is pruned if a threshold proportion of its instantiations in BNC are also instances of the longer child "[dps] point of view." In horizontal pruning, the shorter of the two compared hybrid n-grams is the potentially redundant one and thus the candidate for pruning. As with our MI measure, both vertical and horizontal pruning rate are set post hoc, applied by post-processing, and so are adjustable.

4 Illustrating with Examples

Although StringNet can support a wide range of applications (such as error detection and correction (Tsao and Wible 2009); document similarity measurement, etc.), for ease of exposition in what follows, we take a search query as our access point to illustrate StringNet content. Taking *eye* as our query term, StringNet yields a ranked list of 3,765 hybrid n-grams containing either this lexeme or one of its inflected forms. The following are samples from the top 50 (i.e., the first page of results):

visible [prep] the naked eye
turning a blind eye to
out of the corner of [dps] eye
[dps] eyes filled with tears
keeping an eye on the [noun]
[adv] see eye to eye
look [pers prn] straight in the eye
cast a [adj] eye [prep] (e.g., *cast a critical eye over*, *cast a cold eye on*)

Each hybrid n-gram listed in a search result is accompanied by links to examples and parent and child icons that link to its parent and children hybrid n-grams. (See Fig 1 and 2.) Consider one of the hybrid n-grams listed in the results for *eye*: "keep a close eye on." Recalling Fillmore et al's distinction between substantive and formal idioms, in the case of "keep a close eye on" we are at the level of the formal (lexically filled) idiom. Note that since it is a string of lexical items, as are all substantive idioms by definition, this sort can just as easily be extracted and represented using traditional flat n-grams. StringNet's hybrid n-grams and their cross-indexing, however, allow us to see whether this is a one-off lexically filled idiom or an instance of a lexically open formal idiom (i.e., of a construction). Without hybrid n-grams, the next step up in abstraction to determine this would be pure POS n-grams (strings of POS categories only) used in the literature (Feldman et al 2009; Florian et al 2003; Gamon et al 2009). In the case of "keep a close eye on" the corresponding POS n-gram would be "[verb][det][adj][noun][prep]." This, however, could describe strings as far afield as "buy a new car with" or "sequester the entire jury until." Our hybrid n-grams are intended to address this Goldilocks problem where constructional phenomena fall between these two sorts of traditional n-gram representations evading detection by both.

No	Hybrid ngram	Examples	Parents	Children
1.	**keep** a [aj0] eye on the [nn1]			
2.	**keep** a [aj0] eye on			
3.	[cjc] **keep** a [aj0] eye on			
4.	keep a [aj0] eye on			
5.	**keep** a [aj0] eye on the			

Figure 1: StringNet search interface: "keep a [adj] eye on"

No	Hybrid ngram	Examples	Parents	Children
1.	keeping a [aj0] eye on			
2.	**keep** a close eye on			
3.	**keep** a watchful eye on			
4.	kept a [aj0] eye on			
5.	keep a [aj0] eye on			

Figure 2: Children of "keep a [adj] eye on"

Navigating from "keep a close eye on" upward through the pruned StringNet network using the parent and child links, we find the parent "keep a [adj] eye on" instantiated by attested examples "keep a close/watchful/wary/keen eye on." Another parent of "keep a close eye on" is "keep a close [noun] on".

Tellingly there are only two nouns attested more than once in the noun slot in this frame: "keep a close eye/watch on." Both of these parents in turn share the common parent "keep a [adj][nn1] on." This parent is attested by 268 tokens in BNC. Among these, there are 80 distinct [adj][nn1] pairings filling those two POS slots in this hybrid n-gram (e.g., *close eye*, *firm grip*, *tight rein*, *close watch*, etc.). StringNet allows the extraction of this set of 80 [adj][nn1] pairs and indexes this set to this specific hybrid n-gram. This enables a range of investigations. One direction from here is to explore this particular set of 80 [adj][noun] pairs. For example, we could take this set of pairs as a potential identifying feature set of this construction and search StringNet for other hybrid n-grams with the substring [adj][noun] to identify those that show a large overlap with the 80 pairs from "keep a [adj][noun] on." This would constitute an approach to detecting similar constructions or family resemblances between and among constructions. Another direction is to see whether "keep" is an anchoring lexical element of this construction or substitutable much like the [adj] and [noun] slots. This could be investigated in a number of ways in StringNet. For example, by comparing "keep a [adj][noun] on" with minimally distinct hybrid n-grams with verbs other than "keep," conditional or relative probability measures could indicate whether that set of 80 [adj][noun] pairs from "keep a [adj][noun] on" is conditioned by "keep" or independent of the particular verb in this string.

It's the thought that counts:

For this example, we query StringNet for "count" and get 436 distinct, unpruned hybrid n-grams for the verb. The eight listed below include the top-ranked 5 with 3 others sampled from the top 12, rank order retained:

stand up and be counted
count the number of [nn2]
count [dps] blessings
it **be** the [noun] that **count**
[vm0][adv] be counted as
[pnp] [vm0] not count on
what counts as [nn1]
count [pronoun reflx] lucky

Ranked 4th among these is "it **be** the [noun] that **count**," attested with 21 tokens in BNC. In 9 of these tokens, the [noun] is *thought*, so of course, navigating down we find "it's the thought that counts" as a descendant hybrid n-gram. Numerous aspects suggest themselves. First is the relation between lexically filled substantive idioms and more abstract formal idioms that host them. Starting with the lexically filled "it's the thought that counts" and navigating upward we note that *count* remains specified but can host a range of nouns in the focus position, as indicated by our 4th ranked "it **be** the [noun] that **count.**" The nouns attested in this slot are: *hunt, perception, topic, message, future, critic, change, books, feelings, character, voter, sport*. Upward from here to a proto ancestor, we reach "it be the [noun] that [verb]," a barebones frame of the It Cleft construction and host to the generations of instantiations below it.

Dependency Discovery

In addition to relations among constructions that StringNet encodes, it also yields up internal dependencies between co-occurring grams within a construction. A grand-daughter of the proto "It Cleft" string is telling in this respect: "it **be** the [nn1] that [vvz]". In other words, StringNet here indicates morphological agreement in the "It Cleft" construction. Statistical work on the tokens of these hybrid n-grams can detect such dependencies automatically. Crucially, StringNet provides traction on the grammatical features of quirky aspects of constructions, that terrain between regularity and idiomicity that poses such persistent problems for NLP.

5 Conclusion

StringNet has been created as a resource for investigating constructions and a range of multiple word expressions and for supporting NLP applications that traffic in constructions. While StringNet has been extracted from BNC, we hope that in turn StringNet can provide a richer setting for investigating a range of linguistic phenomena. For example, while computational techniques for extracting collocations have been run on traditional corpora, deeper and more finely nuanced collocation knowledge can be discovered when the larger context of a framing construction is taken into account. Thus not just extracting [adj][noun] collocations, but ones particular to a framing construction or family of constructions. StringNet also renders up grammatical dependencies otherwise hard to detect since they are within the non-canonical structures of constructions. It is hoped that further cross-indexings of StringNet in the future can support increasingly nuanced research on constructions.

Acknowledgments

The work described in this paper was partially supported by the grants from the National Science Council, Taiwan (Project Nos. 96-2524-S-008-003- and 98-2511-S-008-002-MY2).

References

Timothy Baldwin, Emily M. Bender, Dan Flickinger, Ara Kim and Stephan Oepen. 2004. Road-testing the English Resource Grammar over the British National Corpus. In *Proceedings of the Fourth International Conference on Language Resources and Evaluation (LREC 2004)*, Lisbon, Portugal, pp. 2047-2050.

Dwight Bolinger. 1977. Idioms Have Relations. *Forum Linguisticum* 2:157-69.

Dwight Bolinger. 1985. Defining the Indefinable. In Robert Ilson (ed.) *Dictionaries, Lexicography, and Language Learning, ELT Documents 120*. Oxford: Pergamon Press, pp. 69-73.

Gosse Bouma and Begona Villada.2002. Corpus-based acquisition of collocational prepositional phrases. In *Proceedings of Computational Linguistics in the Netherlands (CLIN)* 2001, University of Twente.

Sergey Feldman, Marius Marin, Julie Medero and Mari Ostendorf. 2009. Classifying Factored Genres with Part-of-Speech Histograms. In *Proceedings of Human Language Technologies: The 2009 Annual Conference of the North American Chapter of the Association for Computational Linguistics*, Boulder, Colorado, pp. 173-176.

Charles J. Fillmore, Paul Kay, and Mary Katherine O'Connor. 1988. Regularity and Idiomaticity in Grammatical Constructions: the Case of *Let Alone*. *Language* 64: 501–538.

Radu Florian, Abe Ittycheriah, Hongyan Jing and Tong Zhang. 2003. Named Entity Recognition through Classifier Combination. In *Proceedings of the Seventh Conference on Natural Language Learning at HLT-NAACL 2003.*

Michael Gamon, Claudia Leacock, Chris Brockett, William B. Dolan, Jianfeng Gao, Dmitriy Belenko, and Alexandre Klementiev. 2009. Using Statistical Techniques and Web Search to Correct ESL Errors. *CALICO Journal,* 26(3), pp 491-511.

Adele Goldberg, 1995. *Constructions: A Construction Grammar Approach to Argument Structure*. Chicago: University of Chicago Press.

Ray Jackendoff 1997. The Boundaries of the Lexicon. in M. Everaert, E.-J. van der Linden, A. Schenk, and R. Schreuder, eds., *Idioms: Structural and Psychological Perspectives*, 133-165. Hillsdale, NJ: Erlbaum.

Ivan Sag, Timothy Baldwin, Francis Bond, Ann Copestake, Dan Flickinger. 2002. Multiword expressions: A pain in the neck for NLP. In *Proceedings of the 3rd International Conference on Intelligent Text Processing and Computational Linguistics (CICLing-2002)*, Mexico City, Mexico, pp. 1-15.

Nai-Lung Tsao and David Wible. 2009. A Method for Unsupervised Lexical Error Detection and Correction. *The NAACL Workshop on Innovative Use of NLP for Building Educational Applications*, Boulder, Colorado, pp. 51-54.

Yi Zhang, Valia Kordoni, Aline Villavicencio, Marco Idiart. 2006. Automated Multiword Expression Prediction for Grammar Engineering. In *Proceedings of the Workshop on Multiword Expressions: Identifying and Exploiting Underlying Properties. COLING-ACL 2006*. Sydney. Australia.

Syntactic Construct : An Aid for translating English Nominal Compound into Hindi

Soma Paul
IIIT Hyderabad
soma@iiit.ac.in

Prashant Mathur
IIIT Hyderabad
mathur@research.iiit.ac.in

Sushant Kishore
IIIT Hyderabad
susanta@research.iiit.ac.in

Abstract

This paper illustrates a way of using paraphrasal interpretation of English nominal compound for translating them into Hindi. Input Nominal compound is first paraphrased automatically with the 8 prepositions as proposed by Lauer (1995) for the task. English prepositions have one-to-one mapping to post-position in Hindi. The English paraphrases are then translated into Hindi using the mapping schema. We have got an accuracy of 71% over a set of gold data of 250 Nominal Compound. The translation-strategy is motivated by the following observation: It is only 50% of the cases that English nominal compound is translated into nominal compound in Hindi. In other cases, they are translated into varied syntactic constructs. Among them the most frequent construction type is "Modifier + Postposition + Head". The translation module also attempts to determine when a compound is translated using paraphrase and when it is translated into a Nominal compound.

1 Introduction

Nominal Compounds are syntactically condensed constructs which have extensively been attempted to expand in order to unfold the meaning of the constructions. Currently there exist two different approaches in Computational Linguistics: (a) Labeling the semantics of compound with a set of abstract relations (Moldovan and Girju, 2003) (b) Paraphrasing the compound in terms of syntactic constructs. Paraphrasing, again, is done in three ways: (1) with prepositions ("war story" → "story about war") (Lauer 1995) (2) with verb+preposition nexus ("war story" → "story pertaining to war", "noise pollution" → "pollution caused by noise") (Finin 1980) (3) with Copula ("tuna fish" → "fish that is tuna") (Vanderwende,1995). Nominal compound (henceforth NC) is a frequently occurring construct in English[1]. A bigram or two word nominal compound, is a construct of two nouns, the rightmost noun being the head (H) and the preceding noun the modifier (M) as found in "cow milk", "road condition", "machine translation" and so on. Rackow et al. (1992) has rightly observed that the two main issues in translating the source language NC correctly into the target language involves (a) correctness in the choice of the appropriate target lexeme during lexical substitution and (b) correctness in the selection of the right target construct type. The issue stated in (a) involves correct selection of sense of the component words of NCs followed by substitution of source language word with that of target language that best fits for the selected sense (see Mathur and Paul 2009).

From the perspective of machine translation, the issue of selecting the right construct of target language becomes very significant because English NCs are translated into varied construct types in Hindi. This paper motivates the advantage of expanding English nominal compounds into "paraphrases with prepositions" for translating them into Hindi. The English NCs are paraphrased using Lauer's (1995) 8 prepositions. In many cases prepositions are semantically overloaded. For example, the NC "Hindu law" can be paraphrased as "law of Hindu". This paraphrase can mean "Law made by Hindu" (not for Hindu people alone though) or "Law meant for Hindu" (law can be made by anyone, not by the Hindus necessarily). Such resolution of meaning is not possible from "preposition paraphrase". The paper argues that this is not an issue from the point of view of trans-

[1] Kim and Baldwin (2005) reports that the BNC corpus (84 million words: Burnard (2000)) has 2.6% and the Reuters has (108M words: Rose et al. (2002)) 3.9% of bigram nominal compound.

Proceedings of the NAACL HLT Workshop on Extracting and Using Constructions in Computational Linguistics, pages 32–38,
Los Angeles, California, June 2010.

lation at least. It is because the Hindi correspondent of "of", which is "*kA*", is equally ambiguous. The translation of "Hindu law" is "*hinduoM kA kAnUn*" and the construction can have both aforementioned interpretations. Human users can select the right interpretation in the given context. On the other hand, 'paraphrase with preposition' approach has the following advantages: (a) Annotation is simpler; (b) Learning is easier and (c) Data sparseness is less; (d) Most importantly, English prepositions have one to one Hindi postposition correspondents most of the times. Therefore we have chosen the strategy of "paraphrasing with prepositions" over other kind of paraphrasal approach for the task of translation. The paper explores the possibility of maintaining one to one correspondence of English-Hindi preposition-postpositions and examines the accuracy of translation. At this point it is worth mentioning that translation of English NC as NC as well as different syntactic constructs in Hindi is almost equal. Therefore the task of translating English NCs into Hindi is divided into two levels: (1) Paraphrases for an NC are searched in the web corpus, (2) An algorithm is devised to determine when the paraphrase is to be ignored and the source language NC to be translated as NC or transliterated in NC, and (3) English preposition is replaced by Hindi corresponding postposition. We have compared our result with that of google translation system on 250 that has been manually created.

The next section describes the data in some detail. In section 3, we review earlier works that have followed similar approaches as the present work. Our approach is described in section 4. Finally the result and analysis is discussed in section 5.

2 Data

We made a preliminary study of NCs in English-Hindi parallel corpora in order to identify the distribution of various construct types in Hindi which English NCs are aligned to. We took a parallel corpora of around 50,000 sentences in which we got 9246 sentences (i.e. 21% cases of the whole corpus) that have nominal compounds. We have found that English nominal compound can be translated into Hindi in the following varied ways:

1. As Nominal Compound

   "Hindu texts" → *hindU shAstroM*

   "milk production" → *dugdha utpAdana*

2. M + Postposition + H Construction

   "rice husk"→ *cAvala kI bhUsI,*

   "room temperature"→ *kamare ke tApamAna*

   "wax work"→ *mom par citroM* "work on wax"

   "body pain"→ *sharIra meM darda* "pain in body"

   English NCs are frequently translated into genitive[2] construct in Hindi. In English "of" is heavily overloaded(very ambiguous), so the genitives are in Hindi. The two other postpositions that we see in the above data are *par* "on" and *meM* "in/at" and they refer to location.

3. As Adjective Noun Construction

   "nature cure" → *prAkritika cikitsA*

   "hill camel" → *pahARI UMta*

   The words *prAkrtik* and *pahARI* being adjectives derived from *prakriti* and *pAhAR* respectively.

4. Single Word

   "cow dung" → *gobara*

The distribution of various translations is given below:

Construction Type	No. of Occurrence
Nominal Compound	3959
Genitive(of-*kA/ke/kI*)	1976
Purpose (for-*ke liye*)	22
Location (at/on-*par*)	34
Location (in-*meM*)	93
Adjective Noun Phrase	557
Single Word	766
Transliterated NC	1208

Table 1: Distribution of translations of English NC from English Hindi parallel corpora.

There are 8% cases (see table 1) when an English NC becomes a single word form in Hindi. For rest of the cases, they either remain as NC (translated 43% or transliterated 13%) or correspond to syntactic construct. When NC is translated as NC, they are mostly technical terms

[2]"of" corresponds to "kA/ke/kI", which are genitive markers in Hindi.

or proper names. Our data shows that there are around 40% cases when English NC is translated as various kinds of syntactic constructs such M + Postposition + H, Adj + H or longer paraphrases ("Hand luggage" $\rightarrow$ *hAth meM le jAne vAle sAmAn* "luggage to be carried by hand"). Out of these data, 70% cases are when English NC is translated into M[3] + postposition + H. Thus the translation of NC into postpositional construction is very common in Hindi.

For preparation of test data, we extracted nominal compound from BNC corpus (Burnard et al., 1995). BNC has varied amount of text ranging from newspaper article to letters, books etc. We extracted a sample of noun-noun bigrams from the corpus and manually translated them into Hindi.

In this paper, we propose an algorithm that determines when the syntactic paraphrase of English NC is to be considered for translation and when it is left for direct lexical substitution in Hindi.

3 Related Works

There exists no work which has attempted the approach that we will be discussing here for translating English NC into Hindi. From that perspective, the proposed approach is first of its kind to be attempted. However, paraphrasing English NCs is a widely studied issue. Scholars (Levi 1978; Finin 1980) agree there is a limited number of relations that occur with high frequency in noun compounds. However, the number and the level of abstraction of these frequently used semantic categories are not agreed upon. They can vary from a few prepositional paraphrases (Lauer, 1995) to hundreds and even thousands more specific semantic relations (Finin, 1980). Lauer (1995), for example, considers eight prepositional paraphrases as semantic classification categories: of, for, with, in, on, at, about, and from. According to this classification, the noun compound "bird sanctuary", for instance, can be classified both as "sanctuary of bird" and "sanctuary for bird".

The automatic interpretation of noun compounds is a difficult task for both unsupervised and supervised approaches. Currently, the best-performing NC interpretation methods in computational linguistics focus only on two-word noun compounds and rely either on rather ad-hoc, domain-specific, hand-coded semantic taxonomies, or on statistical models on large collections of unlabeled data.

The majority of corpus based statistical approaches to noun compound interpretation collects statistics on the occurrence frequency of the noun constituents and uses them in a probabilistic model (Resnik, 1993; Lauer, 1995; Lapata and Keller, 2004). Lauer (1995) was the first to devise and test an unsupervised probabilistic model for noun compound interpretation on Grolier encyclopedia, an 8 million word corpus, based on a set of 8 prepositional paraphrases. His probabilistic model computes the probability of a preposition p given a noun-noun pair *n1-n2* and finds the most likely prepositional paraphrase

$$p* = argmaxP(p|n1, n2) \tag{1}$$

However, as Lauer noticed, this model requires a very large training corpus to estimate these probabilities. Lapata and Keller (2004) showed that simple unsupervised models applied to the noun compound interpretation task perform significantly better when the n-gram frequencies are obtained from the web (accuracy of 55.71% on Altavista), rather than from a large standard corpus. Our approach also uses web as a corpus and examines frequency of various preposition paraphrases of a given NC. The next section describes our approach.

4 Approach

This section describes our procedure in details. The system is comprised of the following stages: (a) Web search of prepositional paraphrase for English NC; (b) mapping the English preposition to corresponding Hindi postposition; (c) Evaluation of correct paraphrasing on English side as well as evaluation of translation.

4.1 Paraphrase Selection for Translation

Based on the observation from English-Hindi parallel corpus data that we examined as part of this project, we have designed an algorithm to determine whether an English NC is to be translated as an analytic construct or retained as an NC in Hindi. We used Yahoo search engine to perform a simple frequency search for "M Preposition H" in web corpus for a given input NC. For example, the paraphrases obtained for the NC "finance minister" is given in table 2 and frequency of various paraphrases is shown in the second column:

[3]M: Modifier, H: Head

Paraphrase	Web Frequency
minister about finance	2
minister from finance	16
minister on finance	34300
minister for finance	1370000
minister with finance	43
minister by finance	20
minister to finance	508
minister in finance	335
minister at finance	64
minister of finance	5420000

Table 2: Frequency of Paraphrases for "finance minister" after Web search.

In the table we notice that the distribution is widely varied. For some paraphrase the count is very low (minister about finance) while the highest count is 5420000 for "minister of finance". The wide distribution is apparent even when the range is not that high as shown in following table:

Paraphrase	Web Frequency
agencies about welfare	1
agencies from welfare	16
agencies on welfare	64
agencies for welfare	707
agencies with welfare	34
agencies in welfare	299
agencies at welfare	0
agencies of welfare	92

Table 3: Frequency of Paraphrases for "welfare agencies" after Web search.

During our experiment we have come across three typical cases: (a) No paraphrase is available when searched; (b) Frequency counts of some paraphrases for a given NC is very low and (c) Frequency of a number of paraphrases cross a threshold limit. The threshold is set to be mean of all the frequencies of paraphrases. Each of such cases signifies something about the data and we build our translation heuristics based on these observations. When no paraphrase is found in web corpus for a given NC, we consider such NCs very close-knit constructions and translate them as nominal compound in Hindi. This generally happens when the NC is a proper noun or a technical term. Similarly when there exists a number of paraphrases each of those crossing the threshold limit, it indicates that the noun components of such NCs can occur in various contexts and we select the first 3 paraphrase as probable paraphrase of NCs. For example, the threshold value for the NC *finance minister* is: Threshold = 6825288/8 = 853161. The two paraphrases considered as probable paraphrase of this NC is are therefore "minister of finance" and "minister for finance". The remaining are ignored. When count of a paraphrase is less than the threshold, they are removed from the data. We presume that such low frequency does not convey any significance of paraphrase. On the contrary, they add to the noise for probability distribution. For example, all paraphrases of "antelope species" except "species of antelope" is very low as shown in Table 4. They are not therefore considered as probable paraphrases.

Paraphrase	Web Frequency
species about antelope	0
species from antelope	44
species on antelope	98
species for antelope	8
species with antelope	10
species in antelope	9
species at antelope	8
species of antelope	60600

Table 4: Frequency of Paraphrases for antelope species after Web search.

4.2 Mapping English Preposition to Hindi Post-position

The strategy of mapping English preposition to one Hindi post-position is a crucial one for the present task of translation. The decision is mainly motivated by a preliminary study of aligned parallel corpora of English and Hindi in which we have come across the distribution of Lauer's 8 prepositions as shown in table 5.

The table (Table 5) shows that English prepositions are mostly translated into one Hindi postposition except for a few cases such as "at", "with" and "for". The probability of "on" getting translating into "*ko*" and "of" into "*se*" is very less and therefore we are ignoring them in our mapping schema. The preposition "at" can be translated into "*meM*" and "*para*" and both postpositions in Hindi can refer to "location". However, the two prepositions "with" and "for" can be translated into two distinct relations as shown in Table 5. From our parallel corpus data, we therefore

Prep	Post-Pos	Sense	Prob.
of	*kA*	Possession	0.13
	ke	Possession	0.574
	kI	Possession	0.29
	se	Possession	0.002
from	*se*	Source	.999
at	*meM*	Location	0.748
	par	Location	.219
with	*se*	Instrument	0.628
	ke sAtha	Association	0.26
on	*par*	Loc./Theme	0.987
	ko	Theme	0.007
about	*ke bAre meM*	Subj.Matter	0.68
in	*meM*	Location	.999
for	*ke lie*	Beneficiary	0.72
	ke	Possession	0.27

Table 5: Mapping of English Preposition to Hindi postposition from alligned English-Hindi parallel corpora.

find that these prepositions are semantically overloaded from Hindi language perspective. The right sense and thereafter the right Hindi correspondent can be selected in the context. In the present task, we are selecting the mapping with higher probability. English Prepositions are mapped to one Hindi Post-position for all cases except for "at" and "about".

Preposition	Postposition
of	*kA/kI/ke*
on	*para*
for	*ke liye*
at	*para/meM*
in	*meM*
from	*se*
with	*ke sAtha*
about	*ke bAre meM* *ke viSaya meM* *ke sambaMdhi*

Table 6: Preposition-Postposition Mapping

Post-positions in Hindi can be multi-word as in "*ke bAre meM*", "*ke liye*" and so on. In the present paper we are translating the English preposition to the mostly probable postposition of Hindi. That does not mean that the preposition cannot be translated into any other postposition. However, we are taking the aforementioned stand as an preliminary experiment and further refinement in terms of selection of postposition will be done as future work. For the present study, lexical substitution of head noun and modifier noun are presumed to be correct.

5 Result and Analysis

In this section we will describe results of two steps that are involved in our work: (a) Selection of English preposition paraphrase for a given English NC; (b) Translation of English Preposition to Hindi Post-position.

For a given NC we used a brute force method to find the paraphrase structure. We used Lauer's prepositions (of, in, about, for, with, at, on, from, to, by) for prepositional paraphrasing. Web search is done on all paraphrases and frequency counts are retrieved. Mean frequency (F) is calculated using all frequencies retrieved. All those paraphrases that give frequency more than F are selected. We first tested the algorithm on 250 test data of our selection. The result of the top three paraphrases are given below :

Selection Technique	Precision
Top 1	61.6%
Top 2	67.20%
Top 3	71.6%

Table 7: Paraphrasing Accuracy

We have also tested the algorithm on Lauer's test data (first 218 compounds out 400 of NCs) and got the following results (Table 8). Each of the test data was marked with a preposition which best explained the relationship between two noun components. Lauer gives X for compounds which cannot be paraphrased by using prepositions For eg. *tuna fish*.

Prep	O_{Lauer}	O_{CI}	Percentage
Of	54	37	68.50%
For	42	20	47.62%
In	24	9	37.50%
On	6	2	33.33%

Table 8: Distribution of Preposition on Lauer test data of 218 NC

O_{Lauer} : Number of occurrence of each preposition in Lauer test data

O_{CI} : Number of correctly identified preposition by our method

In Table 9 we compare our result with that of Lauer's on his data. We gave the results with criteria: 1) only "N prep N" is considered. 2) Non-Prepositions (X) are also considered.

Case	Our Method	Lauer's
N-prep-N	43.67%	39.87%
All	42.2%	28.8%

Table 9: Comparison of our approach with Lauer's Approach

Now that we have paraphrased NCs, we attempt to translate the output into Hindi. We *assume* that we have the right lexical substitution. In this paper we have checked for the accuracy of the right Hindi construction selection.

For a given NC we got the paraphrase as "H prep M" or "MH". We use English preposition mapping as described in section 4.2 for translating NC in Hindi. For MH type compounds direct lexical substitution is tried out. We tested our approach on the gold data of 250 Nominal Compounds. We translate the same 250 NCs using google translation system in order to set up a baseline. Google Translator could translate the data with 68.8% accuracy.

Google returns only one translation which we evaluated against our test data. In our case, we have taken 3 top paraphrases as described in section 4.1 and translated them into Hindi by using the English preposition to Hindi postposition mapping schema. The following table presents the accuracy of the translation of the top three paraphrases

Case	Precision
Top 1	61.6%
Top 2	68.4%
Top 3	70.8%

Table 10: Translation Accuracy

In this work we have not considered the context of English NC while translating them into Hindi. Table 11 gives the accuracy of each post-position as translated from English preposition.

The other prepositions have occurred very less in number and therefore not given in the table.

Preposition	Post Position	Accuracy
Of	*kA/ke/kI*	94.3%
For	*ke liye*	72.2%
In	*meM*	42.9%

Table 11: Translation Accuracy for some individual prepositions

6 Conclusion and Future Work

This paper describes a preliminary approach for translating English nominal compound into Hindi using paraphrasing as a method of analysis of source data. The result of translation is encouraging as a first step towards this kind of work. This work finds out a useful application for the task of paraphrasing nominal compound using preposition. The next step of experiment includes the following tasks: (a) Designing the test data in such a way that all correspondents get equal representation in the data. (b) To examine if there are any other prepositions (besides Lauer's 8 preposition) which can be used for paraphrasing (c) To use context for translation.

References

Gildea. D. and Jurafsky. D. 2002. *Automatic labeling of semantic roles*, Computational Linguistics 28 (3), 245-288.

Lapata, M. and Keller, F. 2004. *The Web as a baseline: evaluating the performance of unsupervised Web-based models for a range of NLP tasks.* In: Proceedings of the Human Language Technology conference (HLT/NAACL), Boston, MA, pp. 121-128.

Lauer, M. 1995 *Designing statistical language learners: experiments on noun compounds*, Ph.D. Thesis, Macquarie University, Australia

Moldovan, D. and Girju, R. 2003 *Knowledge discovery from text* In: The Tutorial Proceedings of the 41st Annual Meeting of the Association for Computational Linguistics (ACL), Sapporo, Japan.

Mathur, P. and Paul, S. 2009 *Automatic Translation of Nominal Compound into Hindi.* In: Proceedings of International Conference on Natural Language Processing (ICON), Hyderabad

Moldovan, D., Girju, R., Tatu, M., and Antohe, D. 2005 *On the semantics of noun compounds* Computer Speech & Language 19(4): 479-496

Girju, R. 2009 *The Syntax and Semantics of Prepositions in the Task of Automatic Interpretation of Nominal Phrases and Compounds: A Cross-Linguistic Study* Computational Linguistics 35(2): 185-228

Vanderwende, L. 1995 *The analysis of noun sequences using semantic information extracted from on-line dictionaries* Ph.D. Dissertation, Georgetown University.

Barker, K. and Szpakowicz, S. 1998 *Semi-automatic recognition of noun modifier relationships* In Proc. of the 36th Annual Meeting of the ACL and 17th International Conference on Computational Linguistics (COLING/ACL-98) , pages 96-102, Montreal, Canada.

Finin, T.W. 1980 *The semantic interpretation of nominal compounds* In Proc. of the 1st Conference on Artificial Intelligence (AAAI-80), 1980.

Isabelle, P. 1984 *Another look at nominal compounds* In Proc. of the 10th International Conference on Computational Linguistics (COLING '84), Stanford, USA, 1984.

Kim, S.N. and Baldwin, T. 2005 *Automatic Interpretation of Noun Compounds Using WordNet Similarity* IJCNLP 2005:945-956

Rackow, U., Dagan, I. and Schwall, U. 1992 *Automatic translation of noun compounds* In Proc. of the 14th International Conference on Computational Linguistics (COLING '92), Nantes, Frances, 1992

Learning Rules and Categorization Networks for Language Standardization

Gerhard B van Huyssteen
Human Language Technology Group
Council for Scientific and Industrial Research
Pretoria, South Africa
gvhuyssteen@csir.co.za

Marelie H Davel
Human Language Technology Group
Council for Scientific and Industrial Research
Pretoria, South Africa
mdavel@csir.co.za

Abstract

In this research, we use machine learning techniques to provide solutions for descriptive linguists in the domain of language standardization. With regard to the personal name construction in Afrikaans, we perform function learning from word pairs using the Default&Refine algorithm. We demonstrate how the extracted rules can be used to identify irregularities in previously standardized constructions and to predict new forms of unseen words. In addition, we define a generic, automated process that allows us to extract constructional schemas and present these visually as categorization networks, similar to what is often being used in Cognitive Grammar. We conclude that computational modeling of constructions can contribute to new descriptive linguistic insights, and to practical language solutions.

1 Introduction

In the main, constructionist approaches to grammar focus on discovering generalizations in language by analyzing clusters of usage-based instances of linguistic phenomena. Similarly, computational linguistic approaches to grammar learning aim to discover these very same patterns, using automated techniques such as machine learning (ML).

In this research, we use techniques from ML to analyze and predict irregular phenomena with limited data available, and then represent these phenomena visually in a way that is compatible with the Cognitive Grammar descriptive framework (as a constructionist approach to grammar; henceforth CG). Our grand goal is to develop language technology tools that could be used in descriptive linguistics. Specifically, we aim to (1) develop a predictor that could suggest derivational forms for novel base-forms; and (2) automatically extract categorization networks (i.e. constructional schemas and the relationships between them) from a dataset, which could serve as a heuristic input to descriptive linguistics.

2 Contextualization

This research originates from a practical problem related to language standardization. Similar to standardization bodies for languages like Dutch, and German, the "Afrikaanse Taalkommisie" (TK) is the official body responsible for the description and regulation of Afrikaans spelling. The TK regularly publishes the official orthography of Afrikaans in the form of the *Afrikaanse Woordelys en Spelreëls* ('Afrikaans Wordlist and Spelling Rules'; AWS (Taalkommissie, 2009)).

One of the challenges faced by the TK is to standardize the spelling of foreign place names (including names of countries, cities, regions, provinces, etc.), and their derived forms (i.e. adjectives, such as *Amerika·ans* 'American'; and personal names, such as *Amerika·ner* 'person from America'). In the absence of sufficient usage-based

Proceedings of the NAACL HLT Workshop on Extracting and Using Constructions in Computational Linguistics, pages 39–46,
Los Angeles, California, June 2010.

evidence, many variant forms are often being accepted, either related to spelling or derivation; compare for instance the variant spelling forms *Maskat* or *Masqat* or *Muskat* 'Muscat', or the variant derivational forms *Turkmenistan·i* or *Turkmenistan·ner* 'person from Turkmenistan'. The TK is therefore challenged with the task to give guidelines regarding spelling and derivation, while faced with highly irregular and sparse data containing many variants.

We contribute to address this challenge by discovering the constructions in seemingly unsystematic and irregular data. Based on our tools and outputs, the TK could then revise existing irregularities and variants, or use these tools to guide future decisions.

3 Related Work

3.1 Constructional Schemas

Morphological constructions can be defined as composite symbolic assemblies (i.e. complex form-meaning pairings) smaller than phrases, consisting of component structures between which valence relations hold (Van Huyssteen, 2010; see also Tuggy, 2005). One of the main component structures in morphological constructions is the morpheme, which is simply defined as a simplex symbolic unit in the language system (i.e. it does not contain smaller symbolic units as subparts). More schematic symbolic assemblies (i.e. less specified in their characterization) are referred to as constructional schemas.

Constructional schemas can be represented as a network with relationships of categorization holding between different constructional schemas; these categorization networks provide the structural description of a construction (Langacker, 2008: 222). In the representations used in CG, categorization relationships of elaboration (i.e. full instantiations of a schema), extension (i.e. partial instantiations), and correspondence are specified. Entrenchment and ease of activation is indicated by the thickness of boxes: the thicker the line of a box, the more prototypical that unit is (Langacker, 2008: 226; see also Figure 5).

The aim of descriptive linguistics is to postulate categorization networks that describe a construction in a language, based on usage data. Our research contributes to this aim by automatically creating visual representations of such language models. For our current research, we are specifically interested in the personal name construction in Afrikaans.

3.2 Afrikaans Personal Name Construction

Formation of personal names by means of a personal name creating derivational suffix (NR_{PERS}) is a productive process in many languages. The specific category that we are investigating in this research is personal names derived from place names, such as *Trinidad·ees* 'person from Trinidad'.

In one of the standard works on derivation in Afrikaans, Kempen (1969) identifies a number of NR_{PERS} suffixes that are used in derivations from place names. He finds that there is no obvious systematicity in their distribution (based on a dataset of 132 instances), but concludes that, in derivations of foreign place names, the **-ees** and **-s** morphemes are most frequently used, with some distribution also over **-i**, **-n** (especially **-aan**) and **-r**. In addition to some of the morphemes mentioned by Kempen (1969), Combrink (1990) also mentions a few, while excluding others. In as far as we know, no other description of this construction in Afrikaans has been done, and based on the difference between Combrink (1990) and Kempen (1969), we can also deduct that there is no comprehensive understanding of this construction.

Personal names from place names can be formed in four basic ways in Afrikaans: (1) suffixation (*Aruba·an* 'Arubian'); (2) zero derivation (*Aberdeen* 'person from Aberdeen'); (3) clipping and back-formation (*Turk<Turkye* 'person from Turkey'; *Armeen<Armenië* 'person from Armenia'); and (4) lexicalization (*Cornwallis>Korniër* 'person from Cornwallis'). In a rather large number of cases (119 in our dataset of 1,034; see 5.1) none of the above strategies can be applied, and then paraphrasing is being used (e.g. *'n persoon van Akkra* 'a person from Accra').

Variants of morphemes (i.e. allomorphs) exist for phonological reasons, of which a linking element is the most prominent (Combrink, 1990). Compare for example **-aar** in *Brussel·aar* 'person from Brussels' (where the base-form is polysyllabic) vs. **-enaar** in *Delft·enaar* 'person from Delft' (where the base-form is monosyllabic; *Delftenaar* could therefore also be analyzed as *Delft·en·aar*).

For our purposes, we consider **-enaar** as an allomorph (i.e. elaboration) of **–aar**, and is identified as such in our categorization network (see Figure 5). Similarly, we classify morphemes as allomorphs in cases where an allomorph exists due to identical vowel deletion (e.g. **-an** as a variant of **-aan** when it combines with a base-form ending on an *-a*, as in *Afrika·an* 'person from Africa'), as well as consonant doubling after a short, stressed syllable in the auslaut (e.g. **-mer** as a variant of **-er**, as in *Amsterdam·mer* 'person from Amsterdam').

3.3 Automatic Extraction of Constructional Schemas

Computational modeling of morphology is a vast subfield in computational linguistics, gaining popularity since the 1980s. Pioneering work in the field has been done within the two-level morphology framework, and elaborations on this framework can be considered the basis of state-of-the-art morphological analyzers today. However, since constructing such analyzers manually is hugely expensive in terms of time and human effort, the approach does not scale well for new languages.

To overcome this obstacle, many computational linguists have developed techniques towards the automatic learning of morphology (e.g. Goldsmith, 2001). A key goal is to be able to produce a morphological analysis of the words of a corpus when only provided with the unannotated corpus.

We are interested in the related goal of function learning: given a base-form of a word, learn other forms of the word. Most typically, function learning takes pairs of words (base-forms plus inflected/derived forms) as input to discover patterns in the data. This is also the paradigm used in the current paper.

Several ML techniques have been used to solve specific function learning tasks (such as learning the past tense form of the English verb). Approaches include the use of decision trees, neural networks, inductive logic programming, and statistical approaches (Shalonova & Flach, 2007).

We are not aware of any work related to the automated learning of categorization networks specifically.

4 Approach

Our research has two complementary goals, dealt with separately: (1) to develop a predictor that can suggest potential derivational forms for novel base-forms (and alternative forms for existing base-forms with irregular forms); and (2) to automatically extract categorization networks that are easily interpretable by linguists.

4.1 Prediction of Derivational Forms

In order to analyze existing and predict new derivational forms, we use the Default&Refine (D&R) algorithm (Davel & Barnard, 2004). This algorithm extracts context-sensitive rules from discrete data, and is particularly effective when learning from small training sets. It has the additional advantage that rules generated are interpretable by humans. When applied to the grapheme-to-phoneme prediction task, it has been shown to outperform comparative algorithms (Davel & Barnard, 2008).

The D&R algorithm defines a set of templates and then uses a greedy search to find the most general rule (matching the templates) that describes the training data in question. Examples that are successfully explained by this rule are removed from the data set and the process repeated. Whenever a new rule contradicts examples previously dealt with successfully, these are again added to the training data to be "re-explained" by a later rule. The rule set therefore captures hierarchical default behavior: the last rule defines the default behavior for a specific pattern, and acts as a back-off rule to the second-last (more refined) rule, which would capture deviations from default behavior. The second-last rule would then act as back-off to the third-last rule, and so forth. Rules are therefore explicitly ordered according to the reverse rule extraction order. (The rule extracted first is matched last.)

Once a set of rules have been generated, these describe the training data completely. In addition, by tracing each of the possible rules that may apply to a new pattern (in order), various alternative derivational forms are identified, along with the evidence supporting each option (as in Table 2).

4.2 Extraction of Categorization Networks

While the D&R rules extracted in Section **Error! Reference source not found.** provide a perspective on the phenomena that occur, these rule sets could become extremely large and, accordingly, more difficult to interpret. We therefore attempt to extract categorization networks (*a la* CG) as visual representations in a fully automated fashion. These networks are more easily interpretable, especially to humans.

An iterative string matching process is used to structure "potential morphemes" within a directed tree. Our main assumptions are that:

- the only input to the process consists of a set of unannotated word pairs: base-form + derivational form;
- a morpheme is added as a suffix;
- allomorphs are either shorter than the main morpheme (i.e. characters removed) or longer (i.e. characters added); and
- preference is given to larger strings that occur systematically in the training data.

The following steps are followed:

1. Generate a list of initial *transformation classes* based on the word pairs provided. These are derived through a comparison based on the longest common substring of the derivational form and its respective base-form (see Table 1). The classes specify the character string to be removed from the base-form (if any), and the replacement string; note that ellipses indicates the base-form (or part of it), and curly brackets indicate deletions (i.e. in *China*, delete the *-a*, and then add **-ees**). If a place name and its personal name are identical, the class will be "0".

Table 1: Examples of transformation classes

Place name	Personal name	Class (constructional schema)
Aberdeen	*Aberdeen*	[[x] [0]]
Amerika	*Amerikaner*	[[...] [ner]]
China	*Chinees*	[[...{a}] [ees]]

2. Create a list of all transformation classes and, per transformation class, a set of all derivational forms (referred to as the *transformation derivations set*).
3. For each transformation derivations set, find the largest end-of-word string common to all members of that set (the *set best string*). The set of all "set best strings" are referred to as the *best string list* and can be interpreted as a set of candidate morphemes.
4. For each transformation derivations set, consider the elements in the best string list, and determine if any subsets of the current set exist that match a larger string currently in the best string list. If so, *partition the set into subsets* accordingly. (Each subset is therefore identified by both a transformation class and a best string. For example, three different sets, each with a different best string may be related to a single transformation class. This makes it possible to identify situations where an allomorph is created in other ways than simply adding the morpheme as a suffix.)
5. For each subset, *update the set best string* based on the latest partition; update the best string list to reflect new best strings created.
6. *Repeat* steps (4) and (5) until no further changes are made. The set of morphemes are considered stable, and it now remains to structure these elements into a visual categorization network.
7. In order to create the categorization network, we start with an empty directed graph. For each set best string, create a list of all the transformation classes that are applicable (as calculated above) and *add these transformation classes from largest to smallest* to a single branch of the tree. (One branch is created for each string in the best string list, and is a first attempt at capturing a morpheme along with its different variations.)
8. Consider the nodes at each level (all nodes that have the same node as parent) and wherever one node fully contains another, *move the contained node* to become the parent of the other (cutting the link between the original parent node and the contained node). This process ensures that morpheme candidates that are actually variations of other morphemes are suppressed at each level of the tree.
9. Now *combine* any nodes that occur in different places in the tree but have *identical transformation classes*, by merging the lower node with the higher node. Only identical transformation classes are merged.
10. For each node in the final tree, consider whether the left hand side of the transformation class can be *refined*, specifically by adding additional matching characters based on the final transformation derivations set.

The result of this process is a set of final transformation classes, each describing a constructional schema, and the relationships among these constructional schemas, displayed as a categorization network.

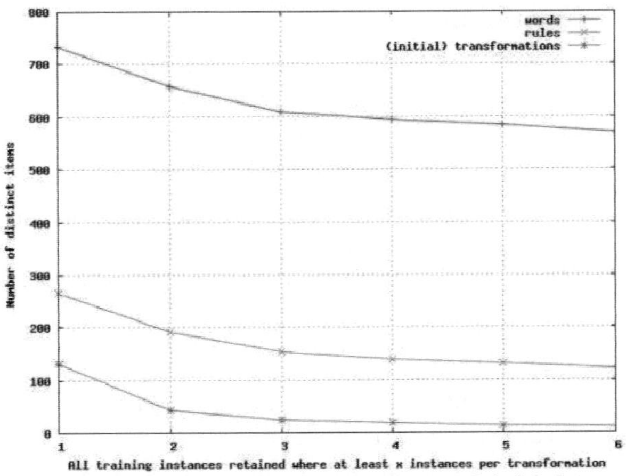

Figure 1: Number of words, rules and initial transformations for the various person-x data sets

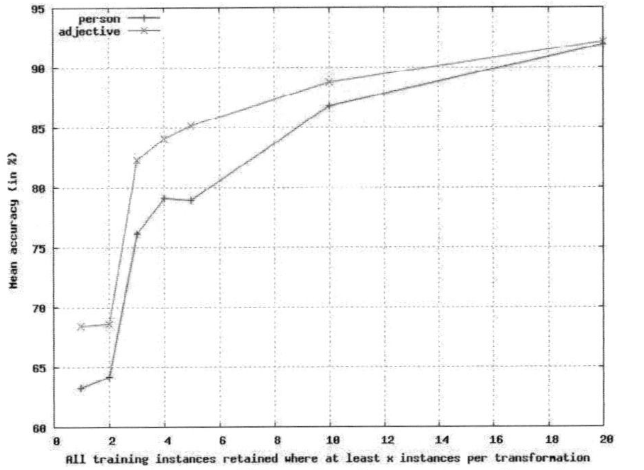

Figure 2: Cross-validated rule accuracy for the person-x and adjective-x data sets.

5 Experimental Setup and Results

5.1 Data

The dataset that we use is the list of foreign place names and their corresponding personal names from the AWS (Taalkommissie, 2009). For purposes of brevity, we only report on suffixation and back-formation, and exclude cases with variant morphemes, zero derivation and clipping, as well as all cases of paraphrasing. 732 instances are retained (from the original dataset of 1,034 instances).

A supplementary dataset consisting of adjectival derivations of place names was also taken from the AWS and treated in the same manner as the personal names; this dataset is used in Section 6.3 to verify certain of the findings. This set contains 786 instances.

5.2 Development of Predictor

The full dataset is highly irregular, containing many transformation classes that occur only once. We are interested in these irregularities (in order to identify words that may need further review), as well as in more systematic phenomena that occur in the data. We therefore create different data sets; in each set (referred to as *person-x*) we only retain those instances that occur *x* or more times in the transformations. (The *person-1* set therefore contains all training data, including all exceptions, while the person-6 set only contains transformations supported by 6 or more instances.) In Figure 1 the number of words and number of unique transformation classes are displayed for each *person-x* data set.

In order to verify the accuracy of our extracted rules, we use 10-fold cross-validation to obtain a mean accuracy per data set, as depicted in Figure 2 (labeled "*person*"). We also generate a rule set from the training and test data combined: this larger set is used to extract categorization networks.

When the rule set is structured as a graph (called a rule network), the data can be interpreted as follows: the root node indicates the default transformation, which applies unless any child node is matched by the base-form, which again only applies unless a child of the child node matches the base-form (and so forth), which indicates that a more refined rule should be applied. A small part of a rule network is displayed in Figure 3, with each node listing the end-of-word string of the base-form that will trigger the rule, the transformation rule that will be applied, and the number of instances of the rule in the training data. The complete rule network is very large: 266 nodes for the *person-1* data set, as indicated in Figure 1.

As was expected, a large number of exceptional rules are generated, indicating much inconsistency in how derivations are formed. For the *person-1* data set, 217 exceptions are identified. For each of these exceptions, alternatives are suggested in order of prototypicality by tracing the rule network, as illustrated for the base-form *Smirna* in Table 2. Automatically generated tables like these provide a practical tool for language standardization.

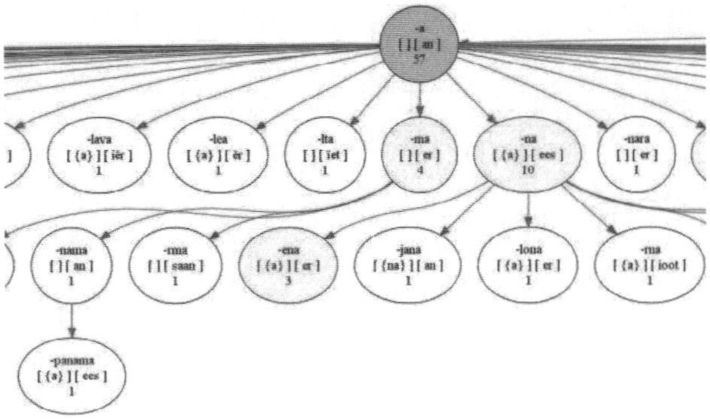

Figure 3: A small subsection of a rule network

Table 2: Alternative suggestions for the exception: *Smirna -> Smirnioot*

Alternative	Instances	Examples
Smirna	*1*	*Smirna>Smirnioot*
Smirnees	*1*	*Navarra>Navarrees*
Smirnaan	*58*	*Sparta>Spartaan* *Astana>Astanaan*
Smirnaer	*155*	*Hiroshima>Hiroshimaer* *Breda>Bredaer*

5.3 Development of Categorization Networks

The categorization network in Figure 5 was compiled automatically, as described in 4.2. Note that this specific categorization network is based on construction schemas with three or more supporting examples per node; for the sake of brevity, we do not include the full categorization network (based on all the examples) in this paper.

The relative prototypicality of constructional schemas (indicated by the thickness of lines in Figure 5) is determined post hoc by observing distribution frequencies. We obtain four natural clusters in this way: highly prototypical (hundred or more instantiations), prototypical (forty or more instantiations), less prototypical (three or more instantiations), and unprototypical (less than three instantiations, therefore also including exceptions); the latter category is not included in Figure 5.

Full instantiations of a schema (i.e. relationships of elaboration) is indicated with solid arrows; the highest node in our network represents the semantic pole, and is here simply indicated as [[PLACE X] [NR_{PERS}]]. For each node in the network, we also indicate the class frequency, and provide three examples of the base-form.

6 Discussion

6.1 Predictor

The extracted rules immediately provide us with:

- An indication of the predictability of the data (rule accuracy);
- A set of all exceptions (single instances that require an individual rule to describe that instance); and
- A predictor of new forms (applying the rules to unseen words).

From the accuracies depicted in Figure 2, it is clear that the full data set, including all phenomena that only occur once, describes a difficult learning task, with an overall accuracy of only 63.2% achieved. When more systematic phenomena are investigated (i.e. transformations with six or more instances), our classification accuracy quickly increases above 80%, indicating that the predictor is in fact usable. An error analysis reveals that improvements may be possible by taking pronunciation information into account (stress patterns, syllable information, consonant categories, etc.).

A standardization body such as the TK could use the automatically generated list of exceptions (similar to Table 2) to review prior standardization decisions. In addition, the predictor can be used to suggest derivational forms for novel base-forms, which could then be verified with usage data.

6.2 Categorization Networks

From Figure 5, observe that we have identified seven basic morphemes (i.e. nodes on the highest level), viz. **-aan**, **-aar**, **-ees**, **-er**, **-i**, **-iet** and **-ër**; with the exception of the latter, all these correspond to the morphemes identified by Kempen (1969) and Combrink (1990). Linguistically speaking, **-ër** is actually an extension of the [[…] [er]] construction, since the e-trema is used in Afrikaans orthography as a variant of the letter "e" to signify a syllable with a null onset, preceded by a syllable without a coda. However, our algorithm treated **-er** and **-ër** as two separate morphemes.

We can also observe that the [[…] [er]] constructional schema can be considered the most prototypical schema (based on frequency). Other prototypical constructional schemas include [[…a] [an]], [[…] [ner]] and [[…] [ër]] (with the latter two actually instantiations of [[…] [er]]). Within a

CG framework, it is assumed that these prototypical constructional schemas are more likely to be activated for the categorization of novel examples.

This observation contradicts Kempen's (1969) finding that there is no obvious systematicity in the distribution of personal name forming suffixes, as well as his finding that the **-ees** and **-s** morphemes are most frequently used. Conversely, we did not find in our data significant evidence for the prominence that Kempen (1969) and Combrink (1990) give to morphemes/allomorphs such as **-der**, **-lees**, **-naar**, **-aner**, **-een**, **-ein/-yn** or **-ioot**; that does not mean that these do not exist – they are just not as prominent as these previous descriptions might have made us believe.

Furthermore, if we look at allomorphs due to linking elements, we identified six, viz. **-nees**, **-enaar**, **-iaan**, **-ner**, **-ter** and **-iër**. With the exception of **-nees**, all these have also been identified by Kempen (1969) and Combrink (1990). If we look closely at the instantiations of [[…] [nees]], we see that all base-form examples end on the stressed syllables [an] or [on], with the exception of *Bali* and *Mali*. A standardization body could therefore investigate whether these two examples could not be classified better under the [[…] [ër]] constructional schema, resulting in, for example, *Bali·ër*, as we also find in Dutch. If this could be the case, then it would make sense why **-nees** has not been identified by other morphologists, since it would then be a case of an allomorph due to consonant doubling, and not due to a linking element.

A similar closer look at **-ees** vs. **-nees** shows that all instantiations of the base-forms of [[…] [nees]] end on a stressed syllable, while those for [[…] [ees]] are unstressed. In the data, there is only one exception to the latter schema, viz. *Gaboen·ees* 'person from Gabon'. Since *Gaboen* ends on a stressed syllable, it would actually fit better under the [[…] [nees]] constructional schema. Support for this hypothesis comes from Donaldson (1993), where he indicates that it should be spelled *Gaboen·nees*. In the absence of usage data, and based on this categorization network, the TK could therefore reconsider the spelling of *Gaboen·ees*.

Several similar observations can be made regarding inconsistencies in the data (e.g. inconsistencies regarding base-forms ending on [stan]). In this sense, categorization networks like these could be a helpful descriptive tool for a standardization body in finding systematicity in data and rules.

6.3 Supplementary Data: Adjectival Derivations

In order to validate the generic process, the full process (as described in 4.1 and 4.2) is repeated using the supplementary data set of adjectival forms described in 5.1. Results are positive: a similarly efficient learning curve is obtained (see Figure 2) and the categorization network, although quite different, is similarly interpretable (Figure 4).

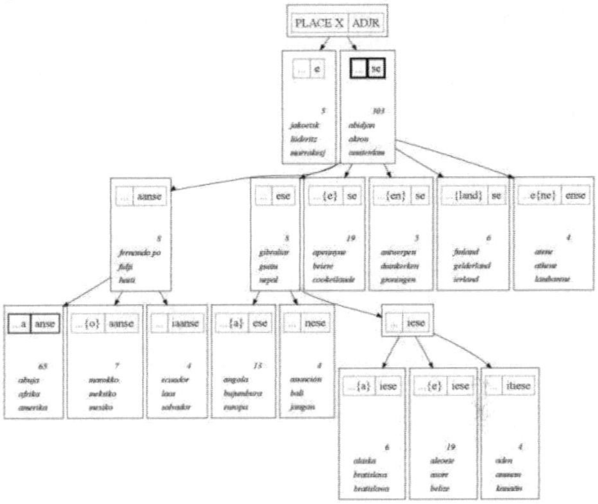

Figure 4: Categorization network for the *adjective-4* data set

7 Conclusion and Future Work

In this paper, we presented a methodology to automatically discover constructional schemas from highly irregular data, and to represent these in a way that is both interpretable by computers (predictive rule sets) and humans (categorization networks). The graphical representation is by and large compatible with one of the major Construction Grammar theories, viz. CG: we show prototypical examples (based on frequency), and also indicate relationships of elaboration. In future work, these representations could be further refined, to also indicate relationships of extensions and correspondences. We have illustrated how these representations could provide insight in our knowledge of the morphology of Afrikaans, as well as providing practical language solutions for language standardization (such as the predictor and the tables with alternative suggestions).

Other future work will continue in two directions: (1) refining the current tool for predicting derivational forms by taking additional features into account, incorporating data that was left out in our current experiments (such as zero derivations), and benchmarking our results with regard to alternative approaches; and (2) applying our algorithm to describe other morphological constructions.

Acknowledgments

Van Huyssteen is jointly affiliated with North-West University. Support by NWU is hereby acknowledged.

Part of this research was made possible through a research grant by the South African National Research Foundation (FA207041600015).

We would like to extend our gratitude to Handré Groenewald and Martin Puttkammer for their help.

References

Combrink, J.G.H. 1990. *Afrikaanse morfologie* [Afrikaans morphology]. Pretoria: Academica.

Davel, M. & Barnard, E. 2004. A default-and-refinement approach to pronunciation prediction. *Proceedings of the 15th Annual Symposium of the Pattern Recognition Association of South Africa*. Grabouw, November 2004. pp 119-123.

Davel, M. & Barnard, E. 2008. Pronunciation Prediction with Default & Refine. *Computer Speech and Language*. 22: 374-393.

Donaldson, B.C. 1993. *A Grammar of Afrikaans*. Berlin: Mouton de Gruyter.

Goldsmith, J. 2001. Unsupervised Learning of the Morphology of a Natural Language. *Computational Linguistics* 27, pp. 153-198.

Kempen, W. 1969. *Samestelling, afleiding en woordsoortelike meerfunksionaliteit in Afrikaans* [Compounding, derivation and change of part-of-speech category in Afrikaans]. Kaapstad: Nasou.

Langacker, R.W. 2008. *Cognitive Grammar: A Basic Introduction*. Oxford: Oxford University Press.

Shalonova, K. & Flach, P. 2007. Morphology learning using tree of aligned suffix rules. *ICML Workshop: Challenges and Applications of Grammar Induction*.

Taalkommissie. (comp.). 2009. *Afrikaanse Woordelys en Spelreëls* [Afrikaans Wordlist and Spelling Rules]. Tenth edition. Kaapstad: Pharos Dictionaries.

Tuggy, D. 2005. Cognitive Approach to Word-Formation. In: Štekauer, P. & Lieber, R. (eds.). *Handbook of Word-Formation*. Dordrecht: Springer. pp. 233-265.

Van Huyssteen, GB. 2010. (Re)defining Component Structures in Morphological Constructions: A Cognitive Grammar Perspective. In: Michel, S & Onysko, A (eds.). *Cognitive Approaches to Word-Formation*. Berlin: Mouton de Gruyter. pp. 97-126.

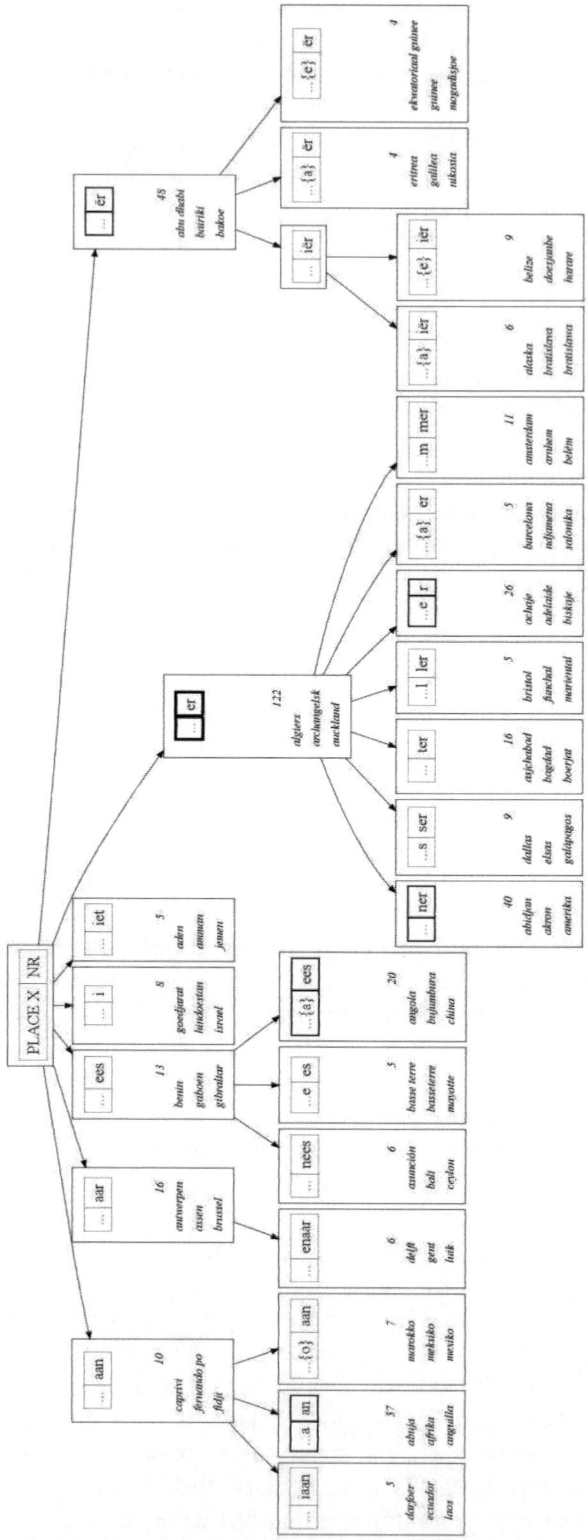

Figure 5: Categorization network for the person-4 data set

Author Index

Association for Computational Linguistics
209 N. Eighth Street
Stroudsburg, Pennsylvania 18360

CURRAN ASSOCIATES INC
proceedings.com